Thomas Arthur Stephens

A Contribution to the Bibliography of the Bank of England

Thomas Arthur Stephens

A Contribution to the Bibliography of the Bank of England

ISBN/EAN: 9783337112189

Printed in Europe, USA, Canada, Australia, Japan

Cover: Foto ©Thomas Meinert / pixelio.de

More available books at **www.hansebooks.com**

A CONTRIBUTION

TO THE

BIBLIOGRAPHY

OF THE

BANK OF ENGLAND.

By T. A. STEPHENS.
(ASSOCIATE OF THE INSTITUTE OF BANKERS.)

Printed at
the Bank of England,
by Walter J. Coe.

TO

A. G. SANDEMAN, Esq.,

GOVERNOR OF THE BANK OF ENGLAND,

THIS CONTRIBUTION

TO THE BIBLIOGRAPHY OF THAT GREAT INSTITUTION

IS RESPECTFULLY DEDICATED.

TABLE OF CONTENTS.

	PAGE
INTRODUCTION.	
BOOKS ON THE BANK OF ENGLAND	1
BOOKS ON THE NATIONAL DEBT .	123
THE FOUNDER. WILLIAM PATERSON	157
THE FIRST GOVERNOR, SIR JOHN HOUBLON	165
THE FIRST DEPUTY-GOVERNOR, MICHAEL GODFREY	166
ABRAHAM NEWLAND .	167
CHRONOLOGICAL SUMMARY OF EVENTS FROM 1694 .	173
INDEX TO NAMES .	183
INDEX TO SUBJECTS	187

INTRODUCTION.

THE following List of Books is the result of a suggestion made to the compiler in 1887 by Mr. H. G. Bowen, then Deputy Chief Accountant, and now Chief Cashier, of the Bank of England. Mr. Bowen's idea was the compilation of a list of publications in the British Museum on the subject of the Bank of England; but the original plan has expanded in the course of execution. In addition to the British Museum, reference has been made to the libraries of the Institute of Bankers, of the City of London, and to that of the Treasury. The compiler takes this opportunity of recording his thanks to Sir E. W. Hamilton, the permanent financial Secretary to the Treasury, for the privileges granted to him there. An attempt has also been made to add to the titles of the books, tracts, and pamphlets that have been mentioned some account of their nature and contents. Generally, the book, or the brochure, has been allowed as far as possible to speak for itself, as it was thought that the weight to be attached to the author's opinions might in some measure be gauged by the way in which he expressed them. In this manner, too, the compiler is best able to avoid the expression of his own views, and to guard against any unintentional misrepresentation of the author's. It would, of course, be quite out of place in a work of this description to ventilate one's own notions, or to discuss moot points in Economics.

This list does not pretend to be a complete bibliography of the Bank of England, but merely a contribution thereto. No one can be better aware than the compiler of its deficiencies. It represents, however, the expenditure of considerable time and labour in the intervals of leisure left by official and other duties during some years, and though it is work that might seem to suffer less than most from interruptions, it has been found that, for several reasons, it would gain greatly by being pursued continuously, instead of intermittently. Such as it is, it is hoped that it may help to supply a want that has been felt by economists and statists, by whom bibliographies of special subjects are much wanted.

No systematic bibliography of the Bank has hitherto been attempted. Indeed, until recently, bibliography has been a comparatively neglected department of English Literature. Now, to workers in historical fields, bibliographies have become an absolute necessity, and as time produces a greater specialisation of work, and makes available a larger mass of material, their value will be enhanced.

As banking is to a certain extent a branch of Political Economy, there is, of course, in works on either subject, a great deal that is common to both. In the bibliography of Political Economy, J. R. McCulloch's "Manual of the Literature of Political Economy," 1845, is the most complete, and, although only including the more notable works, fairly covers the entire subject as then known. In the first and only published volume (A-Cu) of Macleod's "Dictionary of Political Economy," 1863, a list of "Banking Works" is given, but only in a few instances is there any indication of their contents. There are, besides, many interesting and valuable bibliographical notes in the "Dictionary of Political Economy," edited by Mr. R. H. Inglis Palgrave, F.R.S., the publication of which, in parts, was commenced in 1891, and is not yet completed. Bare catalogues of titles and dates are contained also in Lawson's "History of Banking," Jevons' "Investigations in Currency," Thorold Rogers' "First Nine Years of the Bank of England," and in the Appendix to the Reports of the Monetary Conference of 1878, by

Dana Horton. Blanqui, in his "Histoire d'Economie Politique en Europe, &c.," gives a "bibliographie raisonnée des principaux ouvrages," &c.

A bibliography of the Bank is the more needed, as its history from the scientific standpoint of the Political Economist has yet to be written. Francis's History, an excellent work within its limits, deals with the subject rather from the popular point of view. Possibly, if any one endowed with the necessary qualifications for writing a full and exact history of the Bank of England, the literary skill to deal with the vast mass of material, and the historical imagination to give it form and consistency, has ever contemplated the task, he may have been deterred by its magnitude, by the reflection that it must embrace a great deal of the commercial and most of the financial history of the country during more than two centuries. For the literature on the subject is enormous, and as the information it contains has never been collected and exhibited in a systematic form, it is the more necessary that a record of it should be preserved.

The Bank has occupied a high position in national finance from its first establishment, and has had to pay the usual penalty of exalted station. It has been subjected to criticism of all kinds; there has been a tendency to exaggerate its shortcomings, real or imaginary, and a corresponding disposition to decry its merits. It has offered a ready mark to the average currency theorist, frequently a man of one idea, delighted to find fault, and recommending his particular panacea for all commercial evils. But the factors of a financial problem are often far too complex to be distinguishable by the average student, be he theorist or man of business, and the abuse lavished upon the Bank and the Bank system is in many cases simply the result of ignorance.

Such an institution naturally inherits some of the human imperfections of its founders, takes its complexion from its perhaps not altogether healthy environment, and is subject during its growth to the errors and diseases of childhood. To some extent the free development of the Bank has been checked by the circumstances of its origin and early years. It is frequently forgotten that its foundation was due quite as much to the desire of a weak government to strengthen itself, as to any pressing need felt by the commercial world for such an establishment. Till far into the eighteenth century, it acted chiefly as a bank of issue, and as agent for the Government Loans, and had not as yet asserted that banking capacity which was the foundation of its future greatness. There is also this to be borne in mind, that many of the doctrines of Political Economy are still awaiting confirmation, and that to a comparatively recent date, no adequate conception was formed of the far-reaching effects of a motive power of the magnitude of the Bank. Much had really to be decided by "trial and error." It is permissible to say that owing to the introduction of new factors, and the rapid development of banking, the machine had to a great extent to be worked experimentally. Had not the Directors been thorough business men, watching carefully the effect of the Bank's action on the markets, any transient evils would have been fearfully intensified. The Bank, however, has on the whole retained the confidence of the nation at large all through its career, sometimes at considerable self-sacrifice, till the saying, "Safe as the Bank," has passed into a classical English proverb. Every phase in its evolution has been made the subject of keen comment, and often of bitter controversy.

The writer who would undertake a full and exact history of the Bank of England would, of course, look for the material with which to construct his framework chiefly to official sources,—Acts of Parliament, Finance Accounts, Parliamentary Returns, The London Gazette. Most of these are readily accessible, and do not require separate notice. A list of the Acts relating to the Bank of England is quoted in "The Chronological Table and Index of the Statutes." "The Statistical Abstract" of the Board of Trade contains a mass of figures referring to the Bank. Material which vividly illustrates the opinion of the day is to be found in the Reports of Parliamentary Debates, which were more interesting reading prior to the introduction of *verbatim* reporting than they are now. Much valuable information is to be found in the comprehensive Reports of Secret and Select Committees, both of the Lords and Commons, with the evidence on which they are based. Most important among these are the Report of the Lords' Committee on the Order in Council restricting cash payments in 1797; the Second Report of the Committee on Public Expenditure, 1807; the Bullion Report of 1810 (mentioned in the Bibliography); the two Reports on the expediency of the resumption of cash payments, 1819; that on the Bank Charter in 1832; on Banks of Issue in 1840; the two on Commercial Distress in 1848; on the Bank Acts in 1857; and again on Banks of Issue in 1875.

In addition to the Issue of Notes and the ordinary business of a banking house, the Bank of England has, almost from its origin, had the management of the National Debt. In order to give the book some aspect of completeness, notes of a few of the more important works on this latter subject have been added, together with names of some of those less known. Mr. Stutchbury, the Chief Accountant, who has himself written on the subject, has given the writer many valuable hints in respect to this particular portion of the volume, in fact the entire work owes much to his kindly criticism, he having read through the whole of the proof sheets. A great deal of the history of the National Debt is still hidden away in Parliamentary blue books, which are much too numerous to be mentioned separately. Some extremely interesting details of the earliest forms of the Debt are to be found in a return to the House of Commons in 1858, known as the "Goderich Return" (No. 443 of that year), and a further important contribution to its history is contained in the voluminous Parliamentary Return of Public Income and Expenditure, from 1688 to 1869 (No. 366 of 1869). This Return is a vast magazine of information on the financial history of the country, but it sadly lacks an index, although it has a general table of contents, and, at page 313, a very full detailed list of the contents of the "Explanatory and Historical Notices" in appendix 13. Another still more valuable blue book, though, as its title indicates, within much narrower limits, is the "Report by the Secretary and Comptroller-General of the Proceedings of the Commissioners for the Reduction of the National Debt, from 1786, to 31st of March, 1890." This is at present the principal authority upon the history of the National Debt for the period of which it treats. Again, alas! there is no index, but only a table of contents, and a marginal *précis*. The various classes of transactions are, however, distributed into natural and easily intelligible divisions and sub-divisions, and are then treated chronologically.

None of the publications shew the capitalized value of the Terminable Annuities issued by the Government, and it is therefore impossible to make any exact comparison of the total amount of the National Debt in different years. This want has now been supplied, for the last 60 years, in a Return which is annually moved for by the Parliamentary Secretary to the Treasury, and is known in official circles as the "Harcourt Return." It gives the "gross liabilities of the State as represented by the Nominal Funded Debt, Estimated Capital Value of Terminable Annuities, Unfunded Debt," &c., at the close of each Financial Year. The Annuities are capitalized at 3 per cent. to 1888, and thereafter at $2\frac{3}{4}$ per cent. The only attempt that has been made to capitalize the Terminable Annuities from their first issue in 1693, is believed to be that made in the Journal of the Bankers' Institute, for February, 1891, in one of a series of articles entitled "Notes on the National Debt." The Annuities are there capitalized on a uniform basis of 3 per cent., and the total amount of the Debt is shewn for each year of the last two centuries.

While alluding to periodical literature, mention may be made of an article by Mr. R. H. Inglis Palgrave, on "The Price of the Funds and Government Purchases," in the December, 1895, number of the Bankers Magazine.

A few words have to be said about the selection and arrangement of the books. A difficulty in the compilation has been the decision as to what to include. Nearly all the writers of a complete Political Economy, from Adam Smith downwards, have devoted more or less attention to the Bank. Unless, however, they have issued a separate book on the subject, or have given it a special importance, their works have been omitted from the list. These are intentional omissions which any one can supply for himself. Other omissions have been made. The compilation aims at being eclectic rather than inclusive, and where a number of tracts on the same subject, and advocating the same views, have been met with, only those which appear to be the best representatives of the series have been recorded. The publication of the Report of the Bullion Committee, for instance, evoked an enormous outburst of controversial literature—good, bad, and indifferent,—and a selection had almost necessarily to be made. It is to be regretted that so many good tracts have been published anonymously, especially in a subject where the name of a practical man of repute would have given so much additional weight to the opinion expressed.

A word remains of thanks to the present Governor of the Bank, Mr. A. G. Sandeman, for the assistance he has been so good as to afford in allowing the book to be printed at the Bank, and at the Bank's expense. This has necessitated the breaking up of the type as each sheet was approved, and the book is already therefore out of print. A work of this kind is, however, of use only to a small class of persons, and the 250 copies which have been struck off will probably prove sufficient.

T. A. S.

3rd April, 1897.

A BIBLIOGRAPHY

OF THE

BANK OF ENGLAND.

The tracts (1651—1688) marked with an asterisk were published before the foundation of the Bank, and they are given as having contributed, amongst other factors, in no small degree to ripen public opinion as to the expediency of establishing a "General Credit Institution," as it is called by some of the pamphleteers.

1651—1658

* SOME CONSIDERATIONS ON THE TWO GRAND STAPLE COMMODITIES OF ENGLAND and on certain establishments wherein the publick good is very much concerned.

Humbly presented to the Parliament.

By Sir Balthazar Gerbier, Knight. 1651.

One of the earliest tracts on the establishment of Banks in England.

* SEASONABLE OBSERVATIONS HUMBLY OFFERED TO HIS HIGHNESS THE LORD PROTECTOR BY SAMUEL LAMBE, of London, Merchant.
1658.

Describes "a Bank" as "a certain number of men "joined together in Joint Stock," and then goes on to particularize its functions.

B

1660—1682

* AN EXPEDIENT FOR TAKING AWAY ALL IM-
POSITIONS and for raising a Revenue without
Taxes by creating Banks for the encouragement
of trade.
    Francis Cradocke.   1660.

* PROPOSALS FOR INCREASE OF WEALTH BY SUB-
SCRIPTIONS OF MONEY according to the several
particulars herein mentioned, which proposal
having, the 19th May, 1674, been reported to
the Lord Mayor, Aldermen, and Commons in
Common Council assembled, and approved by
them the same was ordered to be published in
the Cities behalf.
    Second Edition.   1675.

* THE MYSTERY OF THE NEW FASHIONED GOLD-
SMITHS, OR BANKERS DISCOVERED.   1676.
    Contains much interesting detailed information.

* CORPORATION CREDIT, OR A BANK OF CREDIT
MADE CURRENT BY COMMON CONSENT, more
useful and safe than money.
    Robert Moray.   1682.

* ENGLAND'S INTEREST, OR THE GREAT BENEFIT
TO TRADE BY THE BANKS, OR OFFICES OF
CREDIT IN LONDON, as it hath been considered
and agreed upon by a Committee of Aldermen
and Commons appointed by the Rt. Hon. the
Lord Mayor, &c.   1682.

* SEVERAL OBJECTIONS SOMETIMES MADE AGAINST
THE OFFICE OF CREDIT FULLY ANSWERED.
                                         1682.

1683—1694

* AN ACCOUNT OF THE CONSTITUTION AND SECURITY OF THE GENERAL BANK OF CREDIT.   1683.

* BANK CREDIT, OR THE USEFULNESS AND SECURITY OF THE BANK OF CREDIT EXAMINED.   1683.

* A MODEL FOR ERECTING A BANK OF CREDIT, &c., &c.   1688.

A BRIEF ACCOUNT OF THE INTENDED B. OF E.   1694.

Most probably by Wm. Paterson, to whom it is attributed by Bannister in his edition of Paterson's works published in 1859 (*q.v.*)

An excellent tract, far in advance of its time, as the following extracts may serve to show:—

" That all money or credit not having an intrinsic value
" to answer the contents or denomination thereof is false and
" counterfeit, and the loss must fall on one or other.

" That the species of Gold and Silver being accepted and
" chosen by the commercial world for the standard or measure
" of other effects, everything else is only counted valuable as
" compared with these.

" Wherefore all credit not founded on the universal species
" of Gold and Silver is impracticable, and can never subsist,
" neither safely nor long, at least till some other species be
" found out and chosen by the trading part of mankind over
" and above or in lieu thereof."

It states that the Bank was strongly opposed by the Jacobites, " who apprehend it may contribute to lessen their " Monarch of France."

1694

SOME USEFUL REFLECTIONS UPON A PAMPHLET CALLED "A BRIEF ACCOUNT OF THE INTENDED B. OF E.," whereunto is annexed a short description of Dr. Chamberlen's Bank.

Second Edition, with Additions. 1694.

The author abuses the intended B. of E. violently, but regains his good humour in giving the Draft of the Land Bank Act, and in raising, and demolishing, imaginary objections thereto, *e.g.*, "This Act will make us all too happy, flourishing "and powerful for all our neighbours, in that it will supply "us at once with as much wealth as the Dutch have been "these many years a raising by their Bank." He hopes this will not be "a sufficient reason why it shall not pass; for "that it will certainly keep out and ruine the French King."

AN ABSTRACT OF THEIR MAJESTIES' COMMISSION UNDER THE GREAT SEAL, dated 15th June, 1694.

For taking subscriptions for the Bank pursuant to the late Act of Parliament.

OBSERVATIONS UPON THE CONSTITUTION OF THE COMPANY OF THE B. OF E., WITH A NARRATIVE OF SOME OF THEIR LATE PROCEEDINGS. 1694.

Complains that the proprietors were not adequately represented, and that a certain Director expected "an unreasonable "reward, ... and in Coffee-houses began betimes to "express himself therein." It is just within the bounds of supposition that this may refer to Paterson, and, if so, it throws some light on the possible cause of his so soon resigning his seat on the Board.

1694—1695

AN INTEREST POCKET BOOK OR TABLES OF INTEREST after the rate of 3, 4½, 5, 6 and 7 per Cent. per annum, from £1,000 to 1s., for any Summ or Time to the Thousand part of a Penny. Exactly computed for the use of the B. of E., and also for any Person that hath Bills or Tallies to discompt.

London printed for the Author, 1694, and sold by Will. Staresmore at the Half-Moon and Seven Stars in Cornhill.

In a copy seen by the writer the following lines occur in MS., date 1712:—

"Gould is uncertaine, but what you possess
Is still your owne, and never can be less."

Also—

"Gold is God with many a one,
But God is God when Gold is gone."

SOME ACCOUNT OF THE TRANSACTIONS OF MR. WM. PATERSON IN RELATION TO THE B. OF E. AND THE ORPHANS' FUND. In a letter to a friend. 1695.

At present the British Museum seem to possess only a fragment of this pamphlet, viz., the title-page.

A SHORT ACCOUNT OF THE B. OF E.

Michael Godfrey (*the First Deputy-Governor*).
1695.

This and Paterson's "Brief Account of the intended " B. of E.," certainly give in a small space the best idea of the Bank's infancy and the more immediate effects of its institution.

1695

First among these effects he places the lowering of interest. He says: "Foreign Bills of Exchange are discounted at £4:10s. per cent. per annum, and Inland Bills and Notes for debts for £6 per cent. per annum, and those who keep their Cash in the Bank have the one discounted at £3 per cent. per annum, and the other at £4:10s. per cent. per annum, for which most Goldsmiths used to take £9 or £10 per cent. per annum, and money is lent on pawns of commodities, which are not perishable, at £5 per cent. per annum, for which some in their necessities have paid more than double as much, to the ruin of many good traders."

He then predicts that the Bank "will reduce the rate of money in England to £3 per cent. per annum in a few years without any law to enforce it."

He cuts hard at the inconvertible currency men. "There are others who are forcing a currency of bills or tallies, and think they may pass as well as Bank Bills, but they do not consider its nothing makes Bank Bills currant but only because that all those who desire it can go when they will and fetch their money for them."

He concludes: "But it may perhaps be objected that the Bank is so far from being an advantage to all trades that 'tis prejudicial to some; for it seems to be admitted that the Bank will be injurious to a dozen or fourteen goldsmiths, and to some scriveners, usurers, and pawnbrokers, because it will hinder them from exacting such oppressive extortion as some of them have done formerly; and it will quite ruin the trade of tally-jobbers.

"Now, if the clamour of a few, whose trade has been to make merchandise of the nation, and to enrich themselves by the necessities of others, shall not only prevail against the benefit of a community, legally establisht, but even of the kingdom in general and the credit of a Parliament, then the enemies of the Bank may hope to subvert it.

1695

"But until the public good be postponed to private
"interest, and a small number of oppressors be too hard
"for the nobility, gentry, and traders of England in
"general, it will and must be preserved and maintained
"because of its great use to the whole realm; and the
"benefits which already accrue by it in its infancy are a
"good earnest of those greater advantages which the nation
"must receive from its future progress."

This tract is quoted in the Report of the Bullion Committee of 1810.

Francis reprints this tract in the appendix to his "History of the B. of E." 1848.

SOME OBSERVATIONS ON THE B. OF E.   1695.

Parts of this little book are very interesting from the historical side, as giving accounts of similar institutions from a contemporary point of view. The following extracts indicate its scope and character.

"The practice of this most excellent constitution the
"Bank hath made a greater progress in a few months
"than could well be expected in several years, being
"naturally so fundamental to the trade and improvements
"of England, it seems to be the harbinger for introducing all
"the excellent things we are capable of, and though it be
"sufficiently able to vindicate itself by the practice thereof,
"and stands not in any need of other, yet because some
"are so very ignorant in things of this nature, and others
"prepossest with notions not only beyond the practice, but
"vastly exceeding all bounds of apprehension, it may be
"of use to give some account of the rise, reason, and use
"of some other Banks in the Xtian world.

"The Bank and Company of St. George in Genoa was
"constituted about the year 1407, when that Government
"was reduced to its worst extremity by war, they were
"obliged to assign over part of their public Revenue to . . . ."
satisfy their creditors, and "to induce further advances,

1695

" and for the better management of this their estate, they
" were erected into a Society or Company with the most
" ample privileges. Thus the Revenue or Estate of
" the Company became prospicuous (!) and transferable,
" answering the use and convenience of money."

This Bank, in a greater degree even than any of the earlier Banks, seems to have had peculiar privileges, their effects being by inviolable constitutions " free from all " manners of arrests, attachments or forfeitures whatsoever, " insomuch that the goods and estates of the worst of " enemies, the vilest of traitors, and the best of friends or " subjects are all alike secure in the Bank of St. George " at Genoa." He goes on to say that it being to the interest of all Governments to support them, they never suffered under any. He then compares it to the B. of E., but prefers the latter. In one year the Genoa Bank took 20,000,000 crowns from the King of Spain in interest alone.

" The Bank of Amsterdam was erected in the year
" 1609, when the Lords of the Government of that City,
" as well to redress the great trouble, loss, and inconvenience
" occasioned by the transportation of great sums of money
" and Bullion of Gold and Silver from one place to another
" in trade, as to prevent and suppress frauds and deceits
" in the weight and alloy of the current money or Bullion
" of Gold and Silver," . . . . do appoint a public deposit
therefor, " with books and registers belonging thereunto for
" transferring or writing off as they call it from one
" account to another."

One function of the Bank was that of a " Clearing " House " of the many different sorts of national coins in which payment was made by the foreign merchants and their agents who frequented the port. It seems if a man had his coin money with him, he paid it into the Bank and received a credit note which was called " Bank Money." All considerable payments were made by this means.

The effects of this Bank were also free from seizure, &c., and the City of Amsterdam took the eventual responsibility.

1695

Then for the practice: "Every one who hath credit "in this Bank brings or sends his order in writing to the "Commissioners to write off from his account, and if any "one leaves the place, he ought to leave a special letter "of attorney with the Bank, constituting some other to "dispose of his interest therein. There have been several "regulations about Bank hours, but that of April 1683 "makes them from 7 to 11 a.m., after 11 a 'late' fee of "6 stivers had to be paid for every writing off or transfer." The Bank shut close at 3 p.m. The "late" fees were devoted to the poor. "Bills of Exchange of 300 guilders "or upward are by law made payable in Bank.

"Thus the Bank of Amsterdam is only a deposit of "ready money for the security of trade and for the con- "venience of writing off instead of paying out, and 'tis "wonderful to think what immense credit this Bank has "acquired in 80 years, it having had upwards of 30,000,000 "Sterling at once." The Bank of Hamburg is said to be similar to the Bank of Amsterdam.

"The obligations of the several provinces and cities of "the United Netherlands cannot be called Banks, because "they are only transferable funds of interest, without a "fund of ready money to supply the occasions of the persons "on demand. But as they are public and obvious estates, "and grounded upon a certain interest, every one's property "therein is always equal to ready money, and have been "of greater use to lower the Interest of Money than any "other constitutions whatsoever." In cities where there were Banks, as, for instance, at Rome, where money was £3 per cent., and at Genoa only £2 per cent., the rates were at least half those of the cities which were not so favoured.

"And it's the happiest art or secret of State that any "people can be blest with, to be able to effect the cure by "the disease, that is, to lower the interest of money by "interest itself."

He goes on to show how Holland had profited by free trade in Bullion, and, contrasting it with Spain, says: "It "should seem that money as well as men inclines to be "where best used and under least restraint."

1695

It is curious that the Bank of Stockholm should have had at this time the National Exchequer work, and that England should have been so late in discarding the cumbersome old machinery, leaving it standing till well into this nineteenth century. *

There is still much that must be left unnoted in this clever tract, which so brightly mirrors forth its times, but space is limited. It concludes with a most able defence of the B. of E., pointing out the fallacies of the Land Bank Scheme with great acumen.

A copy of this book was in William Paterson's library.

---

* Hubert Hall says in his "Antiquities of the Exchequer," published 1891, page 88, " The Chamberlains (of the " Exchequer) were abolished in 1782, and in 1784 the " appointment of commissioners for auditing the public " accounts paved the way for greater changes. Finally, " in 1833, the account side, or the Barons' Chamber, was " swept away, and the lower house or Receipt shared the " same fate. The office of Queen's Remembrancer alone " survived, with the exception of the now obsolete functions " of the Chancellor of the Exchequer as a Baron of the " Court. The practical work of the Exchequer was " henceforth performed by the modern departments of the " Paymaster-General and Treasury itself, whilst the place " of the Receipt was more commodiously occupied by the " Bank of England."

In several of the best tracts of this date, and even fifty years sooner,— for example, by Gerbier, Lambe, and others,— many political truths even now dimly seen, and many grievances, still unredressed, are discussed with the greatest clearness and vigour. Although scarcely within the scope of our subject, it may be noted that there is hardly any respectable tract that does not complain of the difficulty surrounding transactions in the land market in consequence of there being no universal and reliable compulsory registration of ownership, and pointing out the great advantage that the investors in stocks possessed both as to title and readiness of sale or purchase. In these matters the banking world is far ahead of the legal world.

1695 — 1696

REASONS FOR ENCOURAGING THE B. OF E.—

I. In respect of Justice and Common Right.
II. Of its Usefulness and the Publick Good.
1695.

(I.) Argues that the Bank had been granted a charter for eleven years and that it would have been a breach of faith to endeavour to curtail the period; if another Bank were started it would not have so good a credit as the one Bank. (II.) The Bank had been the sole cause of lowering the rate of interest, "and that, too, in time of "war." It had raised the value of tallies from 30 per cent. discount to a premium. It had relieved divers orphans by lending money on the orphan funds at 5 per cent. "It "doth not engross all the money, nor in truth any, being "only a great treasure chest whereinto the subjects put "their money and take it out at pleasure."

The "subjects" no doubt thoroughly appreciated this definition, they, probably, not having forgotten the seizure of the Goldsmiths' cash in the Exchequer by Charles II., by which many of them had suffered great loss.

A SAFE AND EASY METHOD OF SUPPLYING THE WANT OF COIN, AND RAISING AS MANY MILLIONS AS THE OCCASION OF THE PUBLICK MAY REQUIRE, with some Remarks on the B. OF E., &c. 1695.

By the Proposer of the Crown Bank, who abuses other schemes; he, however, finds no fault with the B. of E. beyond stating that it had not yet obtained credit with the Bank of Amsterdam.

THE TRYAL OF THE TRUSTEES OF THE LAND BANK FOR MURDERING THE B. OF E. AT GROCERS' HALL. (1696?)

The humour of this squib is Rabelaisian.

1697

A Discourse of Trade, Coin, and Paper Credit, and of Ways and Means to Gain and Retain Riches. **1697.**

Probably by a lawyer, who seems rather nervous as to the results of an extensive paper currency being issued under a monarchy.

The B. of E. and Their Present Method of Paying defended from the aspersion cast on them in a late book entituled a review of the Universal Remedy for all diseases incident to Coin with application to our present circumstances in a letter to Mr. Locke. **1697.**
By P. H.

The difficulty in getting payment in Coin at the Bank was in consequence of the calling-in of the light gold coin and the inability of the Mint to supply sufficient new coinage. The author says: " So much coin being at " the Mint for recoinage, could the B. of E. make bricks " without straw."

A Reply to the Defence of the Bank: setting forth the unreasonableness of their slow payments. To which is added—

1. The mischiefs that attend the buying and selling of bank notes.

2. The advantages England will reap by having the unclipt hammered money pass current into the Exchequer by weight.

In a letter to his friend in the country. By a true lover of his country and the present Government. **(1697 ?)**

Traverses the statements of "P. H." and blames the Bank, not the Government.

1697 — 1700

THE ARGUMENTS AND REASONS FOR AND AGAINST ENGRAFTING UPON THE B. OF E. WITH TALLIES, &c., as they were debated in a late General Court of the said Bank, considered in a letter to a friend. (1697?)

Maintains that the principal reason against the engraftment was that by so great an enlargement of capital the interest would be out of all proportion to the then profits. He goes on judiciously, however, and shows that this might be overcome by giving the Bank further privileges, one of which was an absolute monopoly, pointing out what a benefit the Bank had been to trade by discounting foreign bills at £3 per cent. for which the Goldsmiths had just before taken £12 and £14 per cent. A clever piece of well-disguised special pleading, worth perusal.

SOME REASONS AGAINST THE CLAUSE RESTRAINING ALL CORPORATIONS BUT THE BANK FROM KEEPING CASH OR BORROWING MONEY PAYABLE AT DEMAND. 1700.

The Sword Blade Co. cries out against the action of the Bank in complaining to the Lord Treasurer of the fact that the Sword Blade Co. had advertized in the Gazette that they lent money.

SOME REASONS OFFERED AGAINST THE CONTINUANCE OF THE B. OF E. in a letter to a Member of the present Parliament. 1700.

One reason is that the Bank absorbs money, and that apprentices out of their time cannot obtain advances to set up with, and that it is dreadful for the Bank to advance money on mortgage and call it in, because the poor freeholder would have either to make repayment or sell his land.

1703—1706

A Collection for the Improvement of Husbandry and Trade.

By John Houghton, F.R.S.

16th April, 1692, to 24th September, 1703.

An extremely interesting set of journals, edited and "run" by Houghton himself, a bookseller. He was a man of very varied attainments, and was one of the first members of the Royal Society; he opens with a flattering testimonial to his own abilities, signed by Samuel Pepys and John Evelyn (both of Diary celebrity), Dr. Hugh Chamberlen (of Land Bank fame), Hans Sloane, and other notabilities of the day. A complete set of these journals in folio form is very rare; most of the other editions are reprints of matter from the body of the publication (which was issued weekly as a rule), consisting principally of technical trade articles on glassmaking, apiculture, &c., &c., and are without the market quotations of Bank Stock, &c., or advertisements, both of which are to the student of finance of the period quite as useful as the "accounts of Earth, Water, Air, and Fire," as Houghton calls them. He frequently ends the weekly numbers with "Next week expect more from "Yours, J. H.," never forgetting to add F. R. S.— (*Vide* Rogers' "First Nine Years of B. of E." 1887.)

Remarks on the B. of E. with regard more especially to our Trade and Government occasioned by the present discourse concerning the intended prolongation of the Bank.

Humbly addressed to the Hon. House of Commons.

By a Merchant of London and a true Lover of our Constitution.

Second Edition.   1706.

An account of the establishment, &c., of the Bank, and a warning as to what an evil it might become under corrupt management.

The author, however, like most of the anti-Bank tractarians, seems unable to bring any specific charge against it.

1707—1711

A SHORT VIEW OF THE APPARENT DANGERS AND MISCHIEFS FROM THE B. OF E., more particularly addressed to the Country Gentlemen. **1707.**

" Would that the Country Gentlemen, as in the good old " days, should make their *diligent* neighbouring tradesmen " their cashiers." The magnitude of the loss entailed by their not doing so may be estimated by the saying of Solomon " that the hand of the *diligent* maketh rich." Complains that the confidence in the security of the Bank, and the temptation of small interest rather than none, make the public prefer to deposit their cash there.

Another edition, 1708, winds up by entreating the " publick not to establish iniquity by a law."

ARGUMENTS AGAINST PROLONGING THE BANK, SHOWING THE DANGEROUS CONSEQUENCES OF IT TO OUR CONSTITUTION AND TRADE, with proposals for advancing the Revenue of the Excise and making it more useful to the Nation than ever the Bank can be, without any danger to the publick. In a letter to a M.P. **1708.**

The author says: " The malignity of the Bank is of " that extent that I know not well where to begin my " account of it."

The Excise duty was payable on quantity, and the brewers universally, after paying it on strong beer, watered the liquor; he proposes to test the quality, and if found inferior to the original sample to double the duty. He prefers this to legalizing "that wen, that wolf of a Bank."

A SCHEME FOR CIRCULATING £1,600,000 IN EXCHEQUER BILLS BY THE MEMBERS OF THE BANK, but separate from the Bank in their politick capacity. **1711.**

This financial puff reads as though written yesterday. It proposes that such members as did not care to subscribe might sell their right of subscription at a good premium, &c.

1712—1717

A Preamble to the Books for taking a Subscription of £1,200,000 for the use of the B. of E. 1712.

A Preamble to the Books for taking a Subscription of "10 Hundred Thousand" Pounds for the use of the B. of E. 1713.

A Preamble to the Books for taking a Subscription of £1,500,000 for the use of the B. of E. 1713–14.

The three preceding papers are practically forms of contract to be signed by the Bank on one hand, and the subscribers on the other.

Rules to be Observed by all Persons that intend to be Subscribers towards Furnishing £1,500,000 to the Bank on a Subscription to be opened 23rd March, 1713.

One rule was "that no person take more than £5,000 "or less than £500."

An Enquiry into the state of the Union of Great Britain, and the past and present state of the Trade and Public Revenues thereof.

By The Wednesdays Club in Friday Street. 1717.

Bannister (1859) gives good grounds for attributing the authorship of these dialogues to Paterson, who, he says, uses the speaker, "Mr. May," to represent himself.

1717—1720

A first series, published some years earlier, deals exclusively with the Union; this set, however, has some extremely interesting passages on the Bank (parts are quoted in the notice of Paterson in this volume), and on the allied subject of the National Debt. The work is composed of a series of reports of imaginary debates of the Club.

The realistic way in which they are written has caused several writers to quote from them as records of actual meetings. Amongst others, the author (Anon.) of the "Theory of Money," 1844, says the B. of E. was invented at the Wednesdays Club, and quotes Allardyce as taking the same view. The individuality of the speakers is remarkably well preserved throughout, and their sayings well and pithily put. Although written by a man who had fought hard, but not always conquered, in the arena of life, they are free from either prejudice or passion.

PROPOSALS OF THE B. OF E. AND THE SOUTH SEA COMPANY as they were delivered to the Hon. the House of Commons stated and compared.
1720.

Showing that the S. S. Co. offered upwards of £2,000,000 more than the B. of E. for the privilege of engrafting the Public Debt on to their Capital Stock.

AN ABSTRACT OF SOME CALCULATIONS relating to the Proposals made by the South Sea Co. and the B. of E. to the House of Commons.
1720.

The "ingraftment" of the Redeemable and Irredeemable Debts would have raised the capital of the S. S. Co. to £43,558,000. The writer asks what trade they could possibly carry on to enable them to pay the interest on so vast a sum, exceeding "the whole of the customs and "excise, much less a farm of them."

The question is ingeniously approached, and seems really to be a *reductio ad absurdum* of the South Sea Co.'s proposals.

1720—1727

The Schemes of the South Sea Co. and the B. of E. as proposed to the Parliament for the Reducing of the National Debts.
1720.

Two proposals from each Corporation, dated January and February, 1719.

Proposals for Restoring Credit, for making the B. of E. more useful and profitable, for relieving the sufferers of the South Sea Co., for the benefit of that of the E. India, and for raising the value of the Land Interest in Great Britain.

Humbly offered to the consideration of both Houses of Parliament. 1721.

Proposes that the Government should issue £10,000,000 paper money to the Bank, who should lend it on mortgage, &c.; in fact a modification of the old Land Bank Scheme.

Suggests £1 and £5 notes, and Branch Banks of England.

An Honest Scheme for Improving the Trade and Credit of the Nation, for punishing the fraudulent and relieving the unfortunate Bankrupts, for increasing the profits of the B. of E., and for paying the Public Debts of the Nation. 1727.

Commences by saying he is very sensible of the bad grace with which all new projects appear in the world since 1720 (S. S. Bubble year).

This tract shows how hardly false ideas die, for "the "honest scheme" is an old friend with a new face, viz., the Land Bank. The idea is that the B. of E. should invest the greater portion of their capital in mortgages, and to facilitate this he proposes the public registry of ownership of land.

1727—1740

He pithily says: "If transfers of land were as easily understood as transfers of stock are, there would be many more purchasers than there now are, which would necessarily raise the price of lands, and I cannot think but 'tis possible to make one as plain as the other."

THE CASE OF THE BANK CONTRACT in answer to the scurrilities of several libels lately printed in the "*Craftsman*." 1735.

This tract, published fifteen years after the bursting of the Bubble, testifies to the violence of the storm which had then raged.

The Contract referred to is that discussed in September, 1720, between the Bank and the South Sea Co., and luckily not ratified by the Bank. The author defends the character of Sir R. Walpole against the imputations of Aislabie, who had been Chancellor of the Exchequer in 1720, and when the crisis came had been compelled to hide himself from the popular fury. He emerged from seclusion in 1735, and grossly slandered Walpole, always herein mentioned as the "Great Person," in italics. Aislabie is described as one "who with unblushing front adds every private immorality to every publick corruption," &c. The courtesies of the press were in no way behind the time.

A DISCOURSE CONCERNING THE CURRENCIES OF THE BRITISH PLANTATIONS IN AMERICA, especially with regard to their paper money, with a P.S. thereto.

Boston, 1740. Reprinted, London, 1751.

This tract deals with inconvertible paper theorists in a way that must have made some of them much regret attacking the writer. He replies to one of them who says "Our paper Bills are a standard for silver": "That is, a ship upon the coast, progressively under sail, stands still while the fields and the trees fluctuate."

1740—1742

Paper money in New England had depreciated 450 per cent., in S. Carolina 700 per cent., and in N. Carolina to the extent of 900 per cent. The Massachusetts people, after long tampering with their currency, postponed levying the taxes, &c., for calling in their paper, for two years, going on progressively till 1722, when payment was deferred till thirteen years later. "To make a Note or "Bill bearing no interest, and not payable till after a "dozen or score of years, a legal ready-money tender "in payment of debts is the highest of despotic and "arbitrary government." Some of the Massachusetts paper of 1717 was still outstanding in 1739, and the price of silver per £ was 29 shillings in paper money. As this paper was originally exchangeable for coin in the year of its issue, State bankruptcy must have hovered very near. He concludes by imploring the Home Government in London, who at this time had the matter under their consideration, not "to use any vigorous sudden methods."

Reprinted in the Overstone collection.

An Appeal to the People of England, the Public Companies and the Monied Interest on the Renewal of the Charter of the Bank. 1742.

Complains that the Bank Stock proprietors were so indifferent that, in order to make up the number constituting a General Court, the Directors were obliged to send specially to some proprietors to come for that purpose.

Some Considerations relating to the intended Bank New Contract. 1742.

Says £3 per cent. was too high an Interest for the proposed advance, as the £3 per cent. Lottery Annuities were then at par.

1746

SIR RICHARD HOARE'S VINDICATION. (1746?)

This "Vindication" is on one side of a single sheet, folio, undated. In Sir Richard Hoare's Journal of his Shrievalty, privately printed at Bath, in 1815, by his descendants, we find that he was knighted 31st October, 1745, the year of his mayoralty, and as he is called "Sir" in the title, and there is mention in the tract of the Life Guards being ordered to march for Scotland, and of "a run on the Bank," one naturally thinks of "'45" and its results. The date of publication might seem, therefore, to have been about 1746. It is here given in full, being of interest as showing the state of public feeling in the City of London at the time of its appearance.

"Whereas there hath been several false and malicious
"reports, industriously spread abroad, reflecting on Sir
"Richard Hoare, Goldsmith, for occasioning and promoting
"a run for money on the B. of E.; in particular, several
"of the Directors of the said Bank reporting, that the said
"Sir Richard sent to the Bank for ten of their Notes of
"£10 each with a design to send several persons with the
"said Notes to receive the money thereon so as to effect
"his ill designs, and to bring a disreputation on the Bank
"and occasion a disturbance in the City of London:—
"This is to satisfie all persons that the Right Hon. Lord
"Ashburnham, father of the Hon. Major Ashburnham,
"Major of 1st troop of H.M. Life Guards, was ordered to
"march for Scotland, sending to the said Sir Richard Hoare
"for a large quantity of Gold and for ten Bank Notes of
"£10 each for the said Major to take with him to bear
"his expenses. The Gold was sent to his lordship
"accordingly, and Sir Richard's servant went to the Bank
"for ten Notes of £10 each which the Cashier of the
"Bank refused to give. But if Sir Richard had intended
"to promote a run for money on the Bank he could have
"done it in a more effectual manner, having by him all
"the time that the great demand for money was on the
"Bank, several thousand pounds in Notes payable by
"the Bank, and also there was brought to Sir Richard
"by several gentlemen, in the time of the run on the Bank,
"Notes payable by the said Bank amounting to a great
"many thousands of pounds which he was desired to take,

1746—1752

" and receive the money presently from the Bank, which
" he refused to do until the great demand for money was
" over.

" N.B.—That the reports against Sir Richard have been
" more malicious than herein is mentioned which he forbears
" to insert for brevity sake."

A Copy of a Letter wrote to a M.P. after the proposals for reducing the Public Debt were rejected at the last General Court of the B. of E., wherein is inserted a copy of the Preamble to the Act of the Ninth Queen Anne for reducing the Interest of Money from £6 to £5 per cent. very proper to be considered by all landed gentry, merchants and traders, especially such as are members of the House of Commons. 1750.

Before the late war it says the £3 per cent. Annuities were £7 per cent. above par, and "at this time the natural
" rate of Interest without the interposition of the Legislature
" is less than £4 per cent.." therefore the Bank might well consent to reduce the rate of interest on the Government Debt. It was reduced from £4 per cent. to £3 : 10s. per cent. in 1750.

" The general legal rate of Interest was fixed in 1714,
" just after Queen Anne's war, at £5 per cent."

Banks and Paper Money, from Essays moral, political, &c.

By David Hume. 1752.

Although perhaps the difference between paper convertible at sight, issued against gold, and inconvertible paper is not so clearly shown as it should be, still Hume is Hume, e.g., " What a pity Lycurgus did not think of
" paper credit when he wanted to banish gold and silver
" from Sparta, it would have served his purpose better
" than the lumps of iron he made use of as money, ...
" and have more effectually prevented foreign commerce."—

Reprinted in the Overstone collection.

1755—1758

Essay on Paper Money and Banking from "Essays on the Public Debt, Frugality, &c." By Patrick, Fifth Lord Elibank.   1755.

The author modestly says that "as the Roman Empire "was saved by the cackling of a goose," he hopes his "own weak endeavours may be successful" in saving his country from financial dangers.

After some stringent remarks on the various disadvantages of paper money, he asks, "Is there no advantage "from this institution of Banks and paper money?" and for answer refers us to "the verses of Mr. Pope,"—

"Blest paper credit! last and best supply!
"That lends corruption lighter wings to fly!
"Gold, imp'd by thee, can compass hardest things,
"Can pocket states, can fetch or carry kings;
"A single leaf shall waft an army o'er,
"Or ship off senates to some distant shore.
"A leaf, like Sibyl's, scatter to and fro
"Our fates and fortunes as the wind shall blow.
"Pregnant with thousands flits the scrap unseen,
"And silent sells a king or buys a queen."

It is a novelty to find Pope quoted as an authority on finance.

Reprinted in the Overstone collection.

Essay of Banks and Paper Credit (from Characteristics of the present state of Great Britain).   1758.

Attributed to Dr. Robt. Wallace, an Edinburgh minister.

Much clearer on the paper money question than Hume, though even here once more crops up the old fallacy of basing an issue on land. "It is of no consequence though "the value of the Bank Notes should happen to extend to "a vast sum provided the Banks which are to answer these "notes have an equal value in coin, lands, goods, and good "debts to which there is convenient access."

Reprinted in the Overstone collection.

1759—1782

HISTORY OF THE PUBLIC REVENUE from 1688 to 1753, with Appendix to 1758.
  James Postlethwayt.   1759.

  Contains "Historical State of B. of E.," giving details of transactions between the Bank and the Government from 1694-1753, alterations in Capital, Stock, and Exchequer Bills circulated by the Bank, together with a detailed account of the National Debt. Quotes Cap. and Sec. of Statutes under which the various operations were effected. Also Historical State of South Sea Co. and the East India Co. for same period in the same detailed manner. A most useful—indeed, invaluable—work to any one writing on these subjects.

UNIVERSAL DICTIONARY OF TRADE AND COMMERCE.
  Malachy Postlethwayt.   1774.

  Very diffuse; contains articles on National Debt, Funds, Public Credit, &c.

THE B. OF E. VADE MECUM OR SURE GUIDE, extremely proper and useful for all persons who have any money matters to transact in the Hall of the Bank, &c., particularly to those who are not practised in that business, in which every office, place, and the manner of procuring Notes of every sort for Cash, or Cash for Notes, is so distinctly described that the greatest Stranger to the Bank may with certainty and propriety do all they want without being obliged to ask any questions of any persons whatever. With two copper plate plans.
  By a Gentleman of the Bank, &c.   1782.

  Sold, amongst other places, at Mr. Pinchbeck's toyshop, Cockspur Street.

  The directions are extremely minute. "Present your
" note to one of the Cashiers through the little rails at one
" of the desks . . . with the words Cashiers wrote against
" the pillars over their heads," &c.

1782—1796

The Drawing, Bill, and Post Bill Offices were then in the Hall, and the Consols Office was split into two sections, A-K in one room, L-Z in another. The Tellers' Office seems to be the only one used for the same purpose now (1896) as in 1782. The plans are quaintly marked, *e.g.*, "Passage " to a back passage," "sham door," "Accomptants," &c. In the Rotunda "The Gentlemen Stockbrokers" assembled from 11 to 1.

REPRINT OF B. OF E. CHARTER OF 1694. Published by Jno. Bell, British Library, Strand. 1788.

SUBSTANCE OF OBSERVATIONS ON THE STATE OF THE PUBLIC FINANCES OF GREAT BRITAIN BY LORD RAWDON (Hastings F.R.) in a Speech on the Third Reading of the Bank Loan Bill in the House of Lords, Thursday, June 9th, 1791.

Contends that the Government was wrong in demanding the Loan of £500,000 on account of Unclaimed Stock and Dividends, as the B. of E. was already in the habit of granting that sum in respect to Exchequer Bills; therefore in demanding the Loan the Government cut their own throats, &c. The Debates on this Bill have been well reported, and are extremely interesting.

A FEW REFLECTIONS UPON THE PRESENT STATE OF COMMERCE AND PUBLICK CREDIT, with some remarks upon the late conduct of the B. of E.

An old Merchant.   1796.

Defends the action of the Bank in restricting the accommodation given to the market, and blames the Ministry.

1797

Substance of the Speech of Sir William Pulteney, Bart., on his motion, 7th April, 1797, for shortening the time during which the B. of E. should be restrained from issuing Cash for its debts and demands. 1797.

After a long criticism on the Bank and its policy, proposes another Bank "whose operations should commence "on the day after the period fixed for the Bank to pay its "Notes in Cash, but not to commence at all" if the Bank "should on that day" pay in cash and continue to do so for a certain time. One can, now, hardly believe Pulteney was serious, and not jesting; the motion, however, was debated, and he seems to have been in earnest, judging from the expressions of the other speakers.

Observations on the Establishment of the B. of E., and on the Paper Circulation of the Country.

Sir F. Baring, Bart. 1797.

Says Sir W. Pulteney's idea of a rival Bank was most unjust, unless the action of the B. of E. could be proved to have caused the panic, which was not the case; the profit on sending bullion to Hamburg in 1796 was £6 to £8 per cent., causing a great exportation of gold thither.

Points out that, in the event of a French invasion and general catastrophe, a B. of E. Note would be still of fair value, because the "Foreigners" knew that to injure the Bank or its credit would be to cut their own throats, and instances the treatment of the Bank of Amsterdam in support of his opinion.

A most valuable and interesting tract.

Further Observations on the Establishment of the B. of E., and on the Paper Circulation of the Country.

Sir F. Baring, Bart. 1797.

Recapitulates the contents of the last tract and insists that some limitation should be placed on the circulation of B. of E. Notes.

1797

LETTERS TO THE GOVERNORS AND DIRECTORS OF THE BANK in September, 1796, &c.
Sir Jno. Sinclair, Bart.   1797.

Suggests various schemes to enable the Bank to continue to pay Cash.

THE HISTORY OF THE B. OF E. FROM THE ESTABLISHMENT OF THAT INSTITUTION TO THE PRESENT DAY, containing a succinct view of the extension of its Capital and Credit; the effects of both: the dangers with which it has been threatened at certain periods, and the measures adopted to maintain the Stability and Credit of it on those occasions: interspersed with reflections of the best financial writers on the subject, with an impartial detail of the proceedings of both Houses of Parliament and the Court of Bank Directors, in consequence of the Order of Council directed to the Governor of the B. of E. on the 26th February last, with the Report of the Committee appointed by the House of Commons to enquire into the affairs of the B. of E. at full length. To which is added a correct copy of the Charter of the B. of E., with the Bye-Laws and other interesting matter.   1797.

A booklet whose principal topic is the panic of 1797. Contains a graphic account of the debate in the House of Commons on the appointment of the Secret Committee, with quotations from the speeches of Pitt, Burke, Fox, and Sheridan. The title-page, which is the most lengthy of any work noticed in this Bibliography, tells all else that needs to be told.

AN ADDRESS TO THE PROPRIETORS OF THE B. OF E. (*suum cuique*).
By A. Allardyce, M.P., one of the Proprietors of the B. of E., 11th December,   1797.

States that the price of Bank Stock had fallen from 220 in February, 1792, to below 120 at the date of this

1797

"Address." Business had, however, during that time been generally good, hence the contention that the "hoard" should not be increased but divided amongst the proprietors, and a detailed account of all transactions and profits laid before them. A bonus, viz., 10 per cent. in £5 per cent. Annuities 1797, was given in 1799.

A CORRECT DETAIL OF THE FINANCES OF THIS COUNTRY, as reported by the Secret Committee appointed by the House of Commons on the motion of the Rt. Hon. Wm. Pitt, &c., &c., to which is added a History of the B. of E.

 By Charles Hales, Author of *Bank Mirror* (1799, *q. v.*)   1797.

A pamphlet of 39 pages.

A SECOND LETTER TO THE RT. HON. WM. PITT, Chancellor of the Exchequer.

 By Edwd. Tatham, D.D., Rector of Lincoln College, Oxon.   1797.

Flatters Pitt grossly and proposes a National Bank, which, with the Mint, would form "together one public "manufactory of currency of both kinds."

IN CONSEQUENCE OF AN ORDER OF H. M. PRIVY COUNCIL, the Governor and Company inform the Bank Stockholders that the Bank is affluent, but that Cash payments are suspended till the opinion of Parliament be taken.

 (Single sheet folio).   1797.

This notice was circulated just before the Suspension of Cash payments which took place on the Order of Council of Sunday, 26th February, 1797. The Bank Restriction Act was passed immediately afterwards.

1799

THOUGHTS ON STATE LOTTERIES.

By a young Gentleman. T. F. Junior. 1799.

One of the innumerable handbooks to the State and other Lotteries.

The author invites persons to buy four copies as a mark of approbation, or two as a mark of disapprobation, and leave their names with the publishers to be printed in the next edition!

THE BANK MIRROR OR GUIDE TO THE FUNDS, in which is given a clear and full explanation of the process of buying and selling Stock in the B. of E., so that any person may become thoroughly acquainted with it in a few hours without consulting a Broker, with an account of the Government and other Securities, a sketch of the History of Commerce, &c.

By Charles Hales. 1799.

A Stockholder's Vade Mecum written in the liveliest style. The scene depicted in the Rotunda, then used as a meeting place by the Consols, &c., Jobbers, contrasts strongly with its present sober aspect.

"A mail come in—What news? What news?—Steady
"—Steady—Consols for to-morrow—Here, Consols—You
"old timber-toe, have you got any scrip?—Here, Scrip!
"Scrip?—Private advices from a wicked old peer in
"disguise—Sold—Shorts—Shorts—" (The Beadle springs
"his rattle to get silence) "—Stop that **** noise! Five
"per Cents—Down—The Pope on his knees—Smoke the
"old girl there in pink shoes?—Madam, do you want a
"Broker!—The French army retreating into—Consols—
"Consols—Up they go—Up they go—You lie, Moses,
"I'd stuff your mouth with pork," &c., &c.

1800—1801

INIQUITY OF BANKING, OR BANK NOTES PROVED TO BE AN INJURY TO THE PUBLIC, and the real cause of the present exorbitant price of provisions. Fourth Edition, Part I.   1800.

In British Museum copy Part II. is wanting. Complains of over-issue of paper by the B. of E. and the country bankers, and says rather oddly, "Whereas farmers formerly "carried purses they now carry pocket-books." Naturally.

A LETTER TO THE RT. HON. WM. PITT on the Influence of the Stoppage of Issue in Specie at the B. of E. on the prices of provisions and other commodities.

    Walter Boyd, M.P.   1801.

Contends the rise of prices was in great part owing to over-issue of Notes by the Bank arising from the Restriction Act.

In 1796 an Association of which Boyd was chairman had proposed a Government Board for the Issue of Promissory Notes payable six months after date of issue, with interest at five farthings per diem (£1 : 18s. per cent. per annum). The Chancellor of the Exchequer, however, substituted the expedient of Funding the Floating Debt by means of a Loan of £7,500,000.

OBSERVATIONS ON THE PUBLICATION OF WALTER BOYD, ESQ., M.P.

    Sir Francis Baring.   1801.

Ably criticises Boyd's scheme, by which more Notes than ever would have been in circulation, as Boyd proposed paying them in Gold, Silver, or *Bank Notes;* under the circumstances the last mode of payment must have been resorted to.

1801—1802

BRIEF OBSERVATIONS on a late Letter addressed to the Rt. Hon. W. Pitt, by W. Boyd, on the Stoppage of Issue in Specie, &c., &c.   1801.

Abuses Boyd as unpatriotic, and says his tract would be read with avidity by the French, as were those of Dr. Price and Lord Stair a few years before.

ESSAI SUR LE CRÉDIT COMMERCIAL.

J. H. M. Marnière. Paris.   (1801?)

Describes the Banks of Genoa and England.

GUINEAS AN EXPENSIVE AND UNNECESSARY ENCUMBRANCE, or the impolicy of repealing the Bank Restriction Bill considered.   1802.

Appropriately, but unconvincingly, quotes Horace, "Quid "juvat immensum te argenti pondus et auri," &c.

The writer, who says he is a barrister, appeals to "plain, unvarnished facts," like all the anti-bullionists. Feels proud of the National Debt being over £500,000,000, and advocates a paper currency with the exception of sufficient coin of low denomination for small change!

CONSIDERATIONS SUR LA FACILITÉ D'ETABLIR À PARIS UNE BANQUE ÉGALE À CELLE DE LONDRES.

J. H. M. Marnière. Paris.   1802.

Insists on the advantages that such a Bank would give to France, especially as regards the war with England.

AN ENQUIRY INTO THE NATURE AND EFFECTS OF THE PAPER CREDIT OF GREAT BRITAIN.
Henry Thornton. 1802.

This interesting tract gives a comprehensive account of the working of the money market at the date of its publication, and of the attitude in which the B. of E. stood towards the rest of the commercial world. As a Bank Director, the author was peculiarly qualified to explain the inner mechanism of the financial system. He insists on the fact of an over-issue depreciating the value of the Note, but does not consider that the Bank Issue was then excessive.

There is an excellent chapter on the Country Banks, in which, whilst confessing their usefulness, he deplores the fact of their eventually having to depend on realising whatever securities they might hold in London so that they might be able to get down gold from the Bank rather than keep their own sufficient gold supply.

Reprinted in the Overstone collection.

CONSIDERATIONS ON THE PROPRIETY OF THE B. OF E. RESUMING ITS PAYMENTS IN SPECIE at the period prescribed by the Act 37 Geo. III.
J. Atkinson. 1802.

Against resumption.

A CONCISE AND AUTHENTIC HISTORY OF THE B. OF E., with dissertations on Metals and Coin, Bank Notes and Bills of Exchange, to which is added their Charter.
T. Fortune. Third Edition. 1802.

He says one of his aims is to "unmask faction," and disclaims any interested motives in his support of the Bank. The Book contains scarcely any solid information.

The rhetoric, however, is amusing, such as (in the largest capitals) :—" The Honour, Stability, and Flourishing " Condition Of That Great And Opulent Corporation," &c., &c.

1803—1804

THE EVENTFUL LIFE AND WONDERFUL HISTORY of that most Notorious Character, Swindler & Forger, Charles Price, commonly called "Old Patch," containing a full account of his unparalleled frauds, impenetrable disguises, and ingenious forgeries during the term of six years on the B. of E. and the public at large.   1803.

Price hanged himself in prison the night before his trial, 4th April, 1786. Although from infancy to sixty years of age a scoundrel of the blackest dye, he escaped punishment till the end. As a record of the criminal life, this chap-book is unique. The story of Price is, however, better told by Francis in his History of B. of E., 1849.

DES FINANCES DE L'ANGLETERRE.
J. H. Lasalle, Paris.   1803.

Comments on the effects of the Bank Restriction Act, and the heavy taxation. He says: "On n'a point oublié "qu'un ministre, Lord Chatham, avona que l'intérêt était "le veritable honneur de la nation brittanique, tandis que "l'honneur était le veritable intérêt de sa rivale."

Many of the foreign tracts of this period are not only valuable for their information, but interesting also from their point of view being opposed to our own.

THOUGHTS ON THE RESTRICTION OF PAYMENTS IN SPECIE AT THE BANKS OF ENGLAND AND IRELAND.
Lord King.   1804.

The Irish paper currency had increased in six years (1797—1803) from £621,917 to £2,633,864, a greater proportionate increase than in England.

"In 1801, 7 per cent. was lost" on all money remitted from Dublin to London, and 18 per cent. on the remittances from Dublin through London to Hamburg.

The rate of Exchange between Belfast and Dublin was against the latter, where only Notes circulated.

1804

At Belfast payments were made in Specie, or in Local Bankers' Notes payable in Cash, and when in Bank of Ireland Notes an additional amount was paid proportionate to the Discount.

The continuance of an unfavourable rate pointed to something more than an adverse Balance of trade, viz., a depreciated currency, especially in Ireland; the only remedy for the evil would be a resumption of specie payments.

Lord King was one of the first to call attention to the real method of proof of the depreciation of a currency and was in advance of Ricardo.

His statement of the case is: "A rise of the Market "or Paper price of gold above the Mint price, and a fall "in the foreign exchanges, beyond the cost of sending "bullion from one place to another, is the proof and the "measure of the depreciation of the paper money."

Although everybody, but the doctrinaire, knows this now, it was many years after 1809 before recognition of "King's law" was general.

A useful Appendix shows the course of Exchange at Hamburg, Paris, and Dublin, and the price of Standard Silver from 1789. This stood at 5s. on 9th February, 1798, and at 6s. 1d. on 8th May, 1800.—(*See* Note, by J. R. McCulloch, to Overstone Tracts, Vol. III., 1857.)

A LETTER TO THE RT. HON. LORD KING in defence of the conduct of the Directors of the Banks of England and Ireland, who his Lordship (in a publication entitled "Thoughts on the Restriction, &c.") accuses of abuse of their privilege, with remarks on the cause of the great rise of the Exchange between Dublin and London, and the means of equalizing it.

Henry Boase. 1804.

Misunderstands King, who is most fair in his treatment of the subject, and states that he has nothing to say against the Bank Directors, but against the Restriction which made it "necessary to repeal the law which prohibited the issue "of Notes under £5," &c., &c.

1805

A Treatise on the Coins of the Realm, in a Letter to the King (Geo. III.) by Charles, first Earl of Liverpool.   Oxford, 1805.

This standard work was reprinted by the Bank in 1880, with the following prefatory note:—

"Bank of England,
"10*th* December, 1879.

"Sir,

"The discussions which have lately taken place on
"International Currency, and the appeals which disputants
"on both sides have made to the 1st Lord Liverpool's Letter
"to the King on Coins, have brought to light the fact that
"the work has been for some time virtually out of print.

"We have considered that we should be rendering a
"service to the public by using some of the means at our
"disposal to republish this valuable treatise which deals
"exhaustively not only with metallic circulation, but also
"with the abuses of which the issue of Paper-Money is
"susceptible.

"We trust that you will signify your approval of this
"measure by permitting us to inscribe this new edition to you
"in your double capacity of Chancellor of the Exchequer,
"and Master of Her Majesty's Mint.

"We remain,

"Your obedient faithful Servants,

"J. W. BIRCH,   } *Governors.*
"H. R. GRENFELL. }

"The Right Honorable
"Sir Stafford Northcote, Bart., M.P."

1805—1807

PRINCIPLES OF CURRENCY AND EXCHANGE.
Sir Henry Parnell. 1805.

ARTICLES OF AGREEMENT which were entered into and mutually agreed upon 12th September, 1764, by and between the Clerks of the B. of E., for the purpose of establishing a fund towards the maintenance and relief of their widows and orphans (amended up to date). 1807.

A copy of this booklet, which was printed by H. Teape, wandered into the British Museum 5th July, 1864, a century from the date of the "Articles." In this copy is inserted a curious table dated 18th June, 1814, showing the premium, or rather the fine, that any member of the widows' fund must pay on marrying a *second* (or third or fourth, as the case might be) wife younger than himself, "calculated at every 5 years of the man's age, and every "year of the woman's age that she is younger than her "husband." A man at 25 marrying a second wife aged 24 paid £2, but if the woman were under 20, £12 : 16s. ! A man of 50 marrying his second wife of 49 paid £3 : 8s., and if she were under 20, £78 : 12s. As the man got older the price rose prohibitively; thus, a man of 75 could marry a lady of 74 for a fine of only £6; if the fair one were but 50 summers, the charge rose to £111 : 8s. If, however, December at 75 would mate with May under 20, he was mulcted to the tune of £190! For the sake of justice it is to be hoped that remittal of premium was made if the lady were older than the clerk; of this, however, no word is said. The original rule was a guinea fine for each year of difference; evidently by this the fund lost, hence this unique table.

AN ESSAY ON THE THEORY OF MONEY AND PRINCIPLES OF COMMERCE.
John Wheatley. 1807.

1808—1810

THE LIFE OF ABRAHAM NEWLAND, late Principal Cashier at the B. of E., with some account of that great National Establishment. 1808.

A capital subject, fertile in anecdote and rich in contemporary history, but very poorly treated. The appendix contains the correspondence between the Government and the B. of E. 1807-1808, a short list of early statutes touching the Bank, with a meagre account of its history.

DESULTORY REFLECTIONS ON BANKS IN GENERAL.
1810.

OBSERVATIONS ON THE PRINCIPLES WHICH REGULATE THE COURSE OF EXCHANGE, and on the present depreciated state of the Currency.

Wm. Blake, F.R.S. 1810.

The advertisement to this treatise is dated May, and the Bullion Report was ordered to be printed 8th June, 1810.

Blake gives a good exposition of underlying principles, and his work must have done much to prepare the public mind for a better apprehension of the Report. In summing up he points out that when the resumption of cash payments did come there would sure to be great lamentation from interested persons, and that there must inevitably be a certain amount of real but transitory evil; still further, that a really healthy state of things could never be established till the day of Cash Payments had returned.

He advised a very gradual contraction of issue until that time, so that the result might be discounted, and a sudden convulsion avoided. The clearness and moderation of this book contrast powerfully with the acrimony and special pleading which pervade the financial tracts of this period.

Reprinted in the Overstone collection.

1810

REPORT, TOGETHER WITH THE MINUTES OF EVIDENCE AND ACCOUNTS FROM THE SELECT COMMITTEE, ON THE HIGH PRICE OF GOLD BULLION. Ordered by the House of Commons to be printed 8th June, **1810.**

This Report, and its Appendices, should be read by all who wish to appreciate the merits or demerits of myriads of tracts published during the "Restriction" time.

Of the 232 pages of the volume, 33 are occupied by the Report itself, 116 are devoted to the Minutes, and the rest to the tables of the course of Exchange and Accounts of Imports, &c., &c.

PRACTICAL OBSERVATIONS ON THE REPORT OF THE BULLION COMMITTEE.
Charles Bosanquet. **1810.**

Differs entirely from the Report, and was the means of calling forth Ricardo's "Reply, &c." (*q.v.* 1811), which McCulloch considers "perhaps the best controversial essay " . . . . on any disputed question of political economy."

Bosanquet was the strongest man of the Anti-Bullionist Party, and in defeating him Ricardo may be said to have gained for the Committee almost entire possession of the field.

OBSERVATIONS ON THE REPORT OF THE BULLION COMMITTEE.
Rt. Hon. Sir John Sinclair.
Second Edition. **1810.**

Thinks the Report was not in accordance with the evidence before the Committee, and too "alarmist" in character considering the exports in 1809 exceeded the imports by £14,000,000, and the Revenue of 1809 that of 1796 by £39,000,000.

This and the preceding tract stand first amongst the numerous Anti-Bullionist publications with which the press teemed at this period.

1810—1811

ANALYSIS OF THE MONEY SITUATION OF GREAT BRITAIN with respect to its Coins and Bank Notes. 1810.

"THE PREFACE EXAMINED, &c." 1810.

A contentious critique of Huskisson's Work on Currency Depreciation. (*q. v.* **1819**.)

THE REAL CAUSE OF THE DEPRECIATION OF THE NATIONAL CURRENCY EXPLAINED and a means of remedy suggested. 1810.

The author failed to see that, at the time, the Bank was really issuing as an Agent for the Government, and proposed an Issue by the Government itself.

A LETTER CONTAINING SOME OBSERVATIONS ON SOME OF THE EFFECTS OF OUR PAPER CURRENCY and on the means of remedying its present, and preventing its future, excess. 1810.

MISCELLANEOUS OBSERVATIONS FOR THE BENEFIT OF THE BRITISH EMPIRE, &c., &c., Remarks on Irish and Scotch Whiskey, a Dialogue between the Emperor Bonaparte and the Author, and Remarks, &c., on the Bank of England.
    A. Balbernie. 1810.

A work original in character from the title-page to the printer's errors.

A SHORT INVESTIGATION INTO THE SUBJECT OF THE ALLEGED SUPERFLUOUS ISSUE OF BANK NOTES, THE HIGH PRICE OF BULLION, AND THE UNFAVOURABLE STATE OF THE FOREIGN EXCHANGE; in two Letters extracted from the *Times* newspaper of the 18th and 20th April, 1811. To which is added the substance of the Earl of Rosse's Speech in the House of Lords on the Exchange and Currency of Ireland, taken from the *Morning Post* of 17th April. 1811.

1811

SUBSTANCE OF TWO SPEECHES made by the Rt. Hon. N. Vansittart, on the 7th and 13th May, 1811, in the Committee of the whole House of Commons, to which the Report of the Bullion Committee was referred. With an Appendix containing the Resolutions moved by Francis Horner, Esq., and the Rt. Hon. N. Vansittart, the Amendments moved by F. Horner, Esq., and various accounts referred to in the Speeches. 1811.

OBSERVATIONS ON THE FALLACY OF THE SUPPOSED DEPRECIATION OF THE PAPER CURRENCY, and Reasons for dissenting from the Report of the Bullion Committee.

    Francis Perceval Eliot.   1811.

A REPLICATION TO ALL THE THEORISTS ON BULLION, COINS, EXCHANGES AND COMMERCE. 1811.

FACTS STATED IN ANSWER TO THE REPORT OF THE BULLION COMMITTEE.   1811.

AN ATTEMPT TO ESTIMATE THE NUMBER OF POOR, 1785–1803, and Observations on the Depreciation of the Currency.   1811.

    An interesting tract.

REMARKS ON THE NEW DOCTRINE CONCERNING THE SUPPOSED DEPRECIATION OF OUR CURRENCY.

    Mr. (*sic*) Boase.   1811.

    Gives *his* nine reasons why the Bank Restriction Act should not be repealed. Anti-Bullionist.

1811

REMARKS ON THE SUPPOSED DEPRECIATION OF PAPER CURRENCY IN ENGLAND. By a Merchant. 1811.

COMMERCE AS IT WAS, AND IS, AND OUGHT TO BE. 1811.

SUBSTANCE OF TWO SPEECHES OF HENRY THORNTON, ESQUIRE, in the Debate in the House of Commons on the Report of the Bullion Committee, on 7th and 14th May. 1811.

An able defence of the Report, and a good general resumé of the subject.

He says: "It was remarkable that when the American "Banks about the year 1720 issued their excessive paper, "the merchants of America attributed the consequent fall "of the Exchange to something in the state of trade."

The Anti-Bullionists did the same, and urged every reason for the unfavourable exchange but the real one—viz., over-issue—which prevented them from seeing the real remedy recommended by the Committee, in a reduction in the amount of paper currency and as speedy a return to Cash Payments as circumstances would allow.

THE SUBSTANCE OF A SPEECH DELIVERED BY LORD VISCOUNT CASTLEREAGH in a Committee of the House of Commons, 8th May, 1811, on the Report of the Bullion Committee. 1811.

Looks at the Restriction Bill of 1797 from the political point of view, viz.—"A surrender for the time of the "sound and legitimate regulations of our ordinary system, ".... to preserve the system itself from destruction." Points out that the attempt to procure Gold to resume Cash Payments would at once make still higher the price of Bullion, and that it was useless to think of Cash Payments till after Peace had been obtained.

1811

SUBSTANCE OF THE SPEECH DELIVERED IN THE HOUSE OF COMMONS BY THE RT. HON. GEORGE ROSE, 6th May, 1811.

A rabid Anti-Bullionist, frequently attributing meanings to his many quotations that they do not bear.

For instance, M. Godfrey, in his "Short Account," &c. (*q.v.* 1695), predicted that the Bank would be able to lower the rate of Interest generally to £3 per cent., as they eventually did; because, however, it was still *legally* at £5 per cent. in 1714, Rose says the Bank entirely failed to fulfil the prediction.

THE HIGH PRICE OF BULLION A PROOF OF THE DEPRECIATION OF BANK NOTES.

D. Ricardo. Fourth Edition, corrected, 1811.

The best account of the scope and purpose of this work is that given in the preface to the third volume of the Overstone Tracts:—

"From 1804 to 1808 inclusive, the market price of gold
" was nearly uniform at £4 per oz., being £2 : 14s. 6d.
" per cent. above the Mint of £3 : 17s. 10½d. per oz., and
" shewing that the currency was depreciated to that extent.

"But in 1809 and 1810 the issues of the B. of E. and
" of the Country Banks were greatly increased, and, in
" consequence, the market price of gold rose, in March,
" 1809, to £4 : 10s. per oz., showing a depreciation of the
" currency of no less than £15 : 11s. 4d. per cent. But
" the real cause of the rise of the market price of gold was
" then comparatively unknown, and the adverse exchange
" with which it was accompanied was ascribed to payments
" on account of the war, the interruption of trade, and so
" forth. . . . In this tract Ricardo showed that redundancy
" and deficiency of currency are only relative terms, and that so
" long as the currency of a country consists partly of gold
" or silver coins, and partly of paper immediately convertible
" into such coins, its value can neither rise above nor fall
" below the value of the metallic currencies of other
" countries by a greater sum than will suffice to defray the

1811

"expense of importing foreign coin or bullion if the currency be deficient, or of exporting a portion of the existing supply if it be redundant. But when a country issues inconvertible paper Notes (as was then the case with England), they cannot be exported to other countries in the event of their becoming redundant at home, and whenever, under such circumstances, the exchange with foreign countries is depressed below par, or the market price of bullion rises above its Mint price more than the cost of sending coin or bullion abroad, it proves that too much paper has been issued, and that its value is depreciated from excess."

The substance of this work originally appeared in the form of letters in the *Morning Chronicle;* the first one was published on 6th September, 1809, being reprinted in book form early in 1810.

These opinions being published before the Bullion Committee sat, no doubt influenced their Report, besides contributing "in no ordinary degree to perfect the theory of money."

Reprinted in the Overstone collection.

Reply to Mr. Bosanquet's Practical Observations on the Report of the Bullion Committee.

David Ricardo. 1811.

McCulloch says, in his notice of this work ('Literature of Political Economy, 1845'), "Ricardo's victory was perfect and complete."

Observations on the Present State of the Currency of England.

Earl of Rosse. 1811.

Anti-Bullionist.

1811

A Letter to a M.P. occasioned by the publication of the Report of the Select Committee, &c.
 J. Atkinson. Second Edition.   1811.

Anti-Bullionist.

Pitt's Bullion Debate. A Serio-comic Satiric Poem.   1811.

A Plain Statement of the Bullion Question, in a letter to a friend.
 Davies Giddy, M.P.   1811.

A temperately written Bullionist tract.

A Letter to Davies Giddy, Esquire, in answer to his plain statement of the Bullion question.
 S. Banfill.   1811.

Sharply written.

The Theory of Money, or a practical enquiry into the present state of the Circulating Medium, with considerations on the B. of E., &c.   1811.

Diffuse.

A Letter to Sir John Sinclair on the subject of his remarks on Mr. Huskisson's Pamphlet.
 By a Country Gentleman. Second Edition.
  1811.

Bullionist.

A Letter to the Rt. Hon. Sir John Sinclair, Bart., M.P., supporting his arguments in refutation of those advanced by Mr. Huskisson on the supposed depreciation of our Currency, including a letter to Sir Charles Price.
 By J. M. Siordet, Merchant, of London.
  1811.

1811

SOME OBSERVATIONS UPON THE ARGUMENTS DRAWN BY MR. HUSKISSON AND THE BULLION COMMITTEE FROM THE HIGH PRICE OF BULLION. (First published in Letters to the "*Times*.")
 By Civis.   1811.

CONSIDERATIONS ON COMMERCE, BULLION AND COIN, CIRCULATION AND EXCHANGES, with a view to our present circumstances.
 By Geo. Chalmers, F.R.S. (Author of the comparative strength of Great Britain).
 Second Edition.   1811.

 Tries to trace the high price of Bullion to other causes than over-issue of paper, is in favour of restriction, and exposes the system of management of the Country Banks, said to be over 700 in number. Useful Appendix, with course of Exchange, &c., &c.

REVIEW OF THE CONTROVERSY RESPECTING THE HIGH PRICE OF BULLION AND THE STATE OF OUR CURRENCY. 1811.

THE SPEECH OF MR. JOHNSTONE on the Third Reading of the Bill for preventing the Gold Coin of the Realm from being paid or accepted for a greater value of such Coin; commonly called Lord Stanhope's Bill. 19th July, 1811.

 Outdoes the Bullionists. Has no dread of a return to Cash payments. "Though the amount now in circulation "be not less than £12,000,000, it would be absurd to "suppose that an immediate demand will be made to the "same extent. Many Notes would still circulate when it "was known that they could be at any time cashed."

 An Appendix, with tables of Imports, &c., and an account of the number of Re-issuable Promissory Notes stamped in England 1805-1810.

1811—1813

Letter to Mr. Huskisson by a Proprietor of Bank Stock. 1811.

The Question Re-stated, in Reply to some parts of "The Question Stated and Examined," in a Letter to W. Huskisson, Esq., M.P. (*See* Question, &c., Huskisson, 1819.) 1812.

Essays relating to Wealth and Currency. J. P. Grant. 1812.

Progressive Value of Money in England. Arthur Young. 1812.

The Lack of Gold. 1812.

Observations on the Circulation of Individual Credit. 1812.

Observations on the Past and Present State of our Currency. 1812.

An Appeal to Common Sense on the Bullion Question. 1812.

Review of the Report of the Bullion Committee. 1812.

Brief Thoughts on the Present State of the Currency of this Country. 1812.

Proposals for Reducing the Price of Silver and for Raising the Value and Diminishing the Amount of our Paper Currency. 1813.

1813—1816

LETTERS ON THE HIGH PRICE OF BULLION IN THE AUTUMN OF 1812, showing the necessity of circulating Bank Tokens at their intrinsic value, and of Repressing Local Tokens. 1813.

A CHART EXHIBITING THE RELATION BETWEEN THE AMOUNT OF B. OF E. NOTES IN CIRCULATION, the Rate of Foreign Exchanges, and the Prices of Gold and Silver Bullion and Wheat, accompanied with explanatory observations.

 S. T. Galton.   1813.

Bullionist.

OBSERVATIONS ON THE EXPEDIENCY AND FACILITY OF A COPPER COINAGE OF A UNIFORM AND STANDARD VALUE ACCORDING WITH THE MINT PRICES OF GOLD AND SILVER BULLION.

 John Grenfell.   1814.

AN ESSAY ON THE INFLUENCE OF A LOW PRICE OF CORN, ON THE PROFITS OF STOCK, &c.

 D. Ricardo. Second Edition.   1815.

PROPOSALS FOR AN ECONOMICAL AND SECURE CURRENCY, with Observations on the Profits of the B. of E. as they regard the Public and the Proprietors of Bank Stock.

 D. Ricardo. Second Edition.   1816.

 Proposed that Bank Notes should be exchangeable for Gold Bars of Standard weight and purity. This plan was tried for a short time on the resumption of Cash payments under Peel, and to some extent checked over-issue, but made the employment of £1 Notes necessary instead of sovereigns; forgeries became numerous, and the old system was reverted to. Also advocated publication of the Bank's accounts for its own sake.

1816

THE SPEECH OF PASCOE GRENFELL, ESQ., in the H. of C., on Tuesday, 13th February, 1816, on certain transactions subsisting between the Public and the B. of E. **1816.**

Thought the Bank overpaid, and moved for a Select Committee of enquiry into the engagements between the public and the B. of E. The Appendix is useful as an index to various printed Reports. The author, in one extract, quotes Mr. Samuel Thornton, at one time Governor, as saying, when a witness before a Committee, "that, as a "high testimony to the good management of the Funds, a "public Loan attempted to be raised, for which the Interest "was to be paid at the Exchequer, entirely failed."

OBSERVATIONS ON THE SCARCITY OF MONEY AND ITS EFFECTS UPON THE PUBLIC.

By Edward Tatham, D.D., Rector of Lincoln College, Oxon. **1816.**

Contends Pitt would have done better to increase the currency than to have formed Sinking Funds. Amongst other things, as sources of Revenue, suggests National Insurance and a Stamp Duty on the circulation of Notes.

The Author appears to have overlooked the fact that an Act imposing a Stamp Duty on the Circulation of Notes had been already passed in 1781, and further Acts on the subject between that date and 1816.

AN ADDRESS TO THE PROPRIETORS OF BANK STOCK on the Management of the Governor and Directors of the B. of E., and on the Laws relating thereto.

Daniel B. Payne. **1816.**

A reasonably written tract in support of the action of the Bank Directors.

1816—1817

A LETTER TO THE EARL OF LIVERPOOL on the cause of the present distresses of the Country, and the efficacy of reducing the Standard of our Silver currency towards their relief.

  C. R. Prinsep.   1816.

REFLECTIONS UPON CIRCULATING MEDIUM, CURRENCY, PRICES, COMMERCE & EXCHANGES, with immediate reference to the present state of the Country.

  Lieut.-Gen. Crauford.   1817.

Bullionist. Canvasses Sir J. Steuart's views, and dares to doubt Adam Smith's dictum, "that the more precious "metal always regulates the value of the inferior in "currency." It is, however, very readable.

A VIEW OF THE NATURE AND OPERATION OF BANK CURRENCY AS CONNECTED WITH THE DISTRESS OF THE COUNTRY.

  W. T. Comber.   1817.

SKETCH OF A PLAN FOR A REFORMATION IN THE SYSTEM OF PROVINCIAL BANKING, by which the Notes of Country Bankers may be rendered as secure as those of the B. of E., and the Agriculturists, Manufacturers, &c., relieved from the Distress and Inconvenience occasioned by the Want of a secure Circulating Medium.

  By a Country Shopkeeper.   1817.

1817—1818

PAPER AGAINST GOLD, containing the History and Mystery of the B. of E., the Funds, the Debt, the Sinking Fund, the Bank Stoppage, the lowering and raising of the value of Paper Money; and showing that Taxation, Pauperism, Poverty, Misery and Crimes have all increased, and ever must increase, with a Funding System.

  William Cobbett, published   1817.

A series of periodical papers, mostly dated 1810-11, written in Newgate State Prison in Cobbett's bitterest manner against the Bank Restriction Act, and republished, with additions, in book form in 1817.

Though their technical value is inconsiderable, they throw a strong light on the internal state of the Country at the time.

A LETTER ON THE PRICE OF THE FUNDS AS CONNECTED WITH THE BANK RESTRICTION ACT.   1818.

A LETTER TO JEREMIAH HARMAN, ESQUIRE (Late Governor of the B. of E.), on the Circulating Medium of the Kingdom and the means of diminishing the practice of Forgery.

  By B. H. C.   1818.

Would prevent forgery by putting the circulation of the small Notes entirely in the hands of private Bankers, as frequent payment into the Bank of their origin, personal interest, and a proposed system of rewards, would frustrate forgery.

TWO LETTERS describing a method of increasing the Quantity of Circulating Money on a new and solid principle.

  Ambrose Weston.   1818.

1818

THE GOVERNMENT AND THE BANK, being a statement of the transactions existing betwixt the Public and the B. of E., contained in Six Letters which have appeared in the *British Press* and *Globe* newspapers. April, 1818.

The title-page bears the following quotation from Mr. Horner's speech in the House of Commons, 1st May, 1816: " A system of profusion on the part of your Government " and of rapacity on the part of the Bank that has no " example in the History of European finance."

A LETTER TO THE PROPRIETORS OF THE B. of E. on the Division of the Surplus Profits of that Corporation.

By Charles Arnott, Solicitor, September, 1818.

Relates to the proceedings taking place on the Court of Queen's Bench granting a rule to show cause why a Mandamus should not be directed to the B. of E. commanding them to divide all undivided profits up to 19th March, 1818. The original affidavit was filed by Nathaniel Gundry, a Bank Stock proprietor, who, not having used all possible means provided for in the Charter, &c., to gain his end, before applying to the Court, lost his case, Lord Ellenborough, C. J., observing that Mr. Gundry " should have submitted a motion to the competent authority " that there should be laid before the Court the information " required, and if that Motion was not complied with, then " there might be a Mandamus to compel the Directors to " render such an account." This tract quotes the opinion of Sir James Mansfield, who was consulted by Allardyce (*q. v.*) in **1801**. A Bonus of 25 per cent. Stock had been declared in 1816, only two years before.

1818—1819

A Plain Narrative of Transactions as they relate to a Post Bill of Fifty Pounds, detained at the B. of E., containing copies of a Memorial and Five Letters to the Governor and Directors of the Bank, and the answers of Messrs. Kaye, Freshfield & Kaye, their Solicitors. Published as a Caution to the Merchants and Traders of Great Britain, and with a view to obtain, for the Author, Legal Remedial Advice.

By Benjamin Smart, Refiner and Dealer in Foreign Coin, 55, Prince's St., Leicester Square.

1818.

Smart had a grievance against the Bank in respect to a Bank Post Bill of £50; he here gives the details of the dispute.

The Question of the Depreciation of the Currency Stated and Explained.

W. Huskisson. (New Edition.) 1819.

Originally published 1810-11.

One of the best books by one of the best of the Bullionists; nothing can be more lucid or forcible than the following general statement of the case:—

"Any Bank of which the profits are proportionate to
"the amount of its issues, and which has nothing to
"consider, in making these issues, but the quality and
"character of the securities upon which its loans are advanced,
"must have a natural tendency to a continual increase of its
"paper. It appears to me, therefore, extremely probable
"that for some considerable time before the depreciation of
"our paper currency was materially marked by the high
"price of gold bullion, the amount of Bank issues was in
"excess. But the full effect of this excess was not so
"sensibly felt because, so long as our currency consisted
"of a mixture of gold and paper, the former would give
"way, and either be exported or melted down, and by

1819

"thus gradually making room for the augmentation of
" paper, the value of the latter would be, in a great degree,
" sustained. But when, by these successive additions to
" the amount of the B. of E. and Country paper, nearly
" the whole of the gold had been shoved out of circulation,
" whilst the same disposition and motives to increase the
" issue of paper still continued, the effect of any such
" further increase would be more rapidly and seriously felt
" in the diminished value of our remaining currency.—By
" an unfortunate coincidence of circumstances, a disposition
" to apply for a great increase of discounts was excited in
" the mercantile world much about the same time when
" the greatest part of our gold had been driven away; the
" facility with which these discounts were effected must
" have contributed in this state of things to accelerate the
" depreciation of our currency."

His whole exposition of the subject is most masterly.

Reprinted in the Overstone collection.

A PLAIN STATEMENT OF THE BULLION QUESTION, in a letter to a friend.

Davies Gilbert, M.P. Second Edition.

1819.

A Bullionist. A moderately written tract by a competent man.

THE REAL CAUSE OF THE INCREASED PRICE OF THE NECESSARIES OF LIFE, AND THE HIGH PRICE OF GOLD BULLION.

Edward Cooke. 1819.

Anti-Bullionist, quiet in tone.

SUBSTANCE OF THE SPEECH OF LORD LIVERPOOL ON THE REPORT OF THE BANK COMMITTEE.

1819.

1819

REPRESENTATION AGREED UPON 20TH MAY, 1819, BY THE DIRECTORS OF THE B. OF E., AND HEARD BEFORE THE CHANCELLOR OF THE EXCHEQUER.

The Bank reasonably suggested that as they were to provide bullion for the resumption of Cash payments, the State might repay them some of the advances which had been made on Exchequer Bills, and urged that however much dirt had been thrown at them, they had come out before the Committee with clean hands.

DANGERS OF AN ENTIRE REPEAL OF THE BANK RESTRICTION ACT, and a plan for obviating them.

John Wray. (1819?)

Questions if there were a sufficiency of gold for resumption of Cash payments, and canvasses various expedients to keep the gold in the country.

THE TRUE CAUSE OF DEPRECIATION TRACED TO THE STATE OF OUR SILVER CURRENCY.

A. W. Rutherford. 1819.

A FEW REMARKS ON THE REPORTS OF THE COMMITTEES ON THE CURRENCY, &c., &c.
AND 1819.
FURTHER REMARKS, &c. By the Author of a "Few Remarks, &c." 1819.

Two rather amusing tracts.

The author terms Hume "that elegant but hollow writer," because it had been asserted, on Hume's authority, that a diminution of currency increases its value.

In a remarkable attempt at a *reductio ad absurdum*, he argues that if lessening the paper currency brings down the price of gold, then the price of gold and of all other articles might gradually be brought down to nothing!

1819

AN ADDRESS TO THE RT. HON. ROBT. PEEL, Late Chairman to the Committee on the Currency.
Thomas Smith, Accountant. 1819.

A LETTER TO THE RT. HON. ROBERT PEEL, M.P. for the University of Oxford, on the pernicious effects of a Variable Standard of Value, especially as it regards the condition of the lower Orders and the Poor Laws.
By one of his Constituents. 1819.

A REPLY TO THE AUTHOR OF A LETTER TO THE RT. HON. ROBERT PEEL on the pernicious effects of a Variable Standard of Value. 1819.

REMARKS ON SOME OCCURRENCES SINCE THE REPORTS OF THE COMMITTEES, &c., &c., and on the expediency of the resumption of Cash Payments at the B. of E. 1819.

Scarcely worth reading. The Reports themselves are, as a rule, superior in every respect to the tracts.

The latter, in the majority of cases, reflect the crass way in which the public, for the most part, regarded the questions at issue.

THOUGHTS ON THE RESUMPTION OF CASH PAYMENTS BY THE B. OF E., &c., &c., in a letter to the Chancellor of the Exchequer.
A. H. Chambers, Banker, Bond Street. 1819.

Asserts that the Bank should not resume Cash payments till the price of Gold be brought down to 77s. 10½d. "This would probably be brought about by raising the "importation price of corn to 90s. or 100s., thus encouraging "the farmer to employ those individuals now on the Poor "Rates."

Now (77 years later) we can say that the Mint price of Gold is 77s. 10½d. although the price of Corn is not 90s.

1819

AN ADDRESS TO THE PUBLIC ON THE PLAN PROPOSED BY THE SECRET COMMITTEE OF THE HOUSE OF COMMONS FOR EXAMINING THE AFFAIRS OF THE BANK.
Edward Cooke. 1819.

Anti-Bullionist.

A SECOND LETTER TO THE EARL OF LIVERPOOL ON THE BANK REPORTS AS OCCASIONING THE NATIONAL DANGERS AND DISTRESSES.
Thomas Attwood. 1819.

Believes resumption of Cash payments to mean "Anarchy, "Revolution, Death." The effects of the Resumption, so long foreseen, must have been discounted, especially by the more prudent, and although there was a panic in 1825, it was principally caused by the excessive issue of the Country Banks, which, in 1825, was 50 per cent. more than in 1822.

A LETTER TO THOMAS BRAND, M.P., &c., &c., ON THE RESUMPTION OF SPECIE PAYMENTS.
E. Bollmann, M.D. 1819.

Anti-Bullionist.

PROOFS OF THE IMPRACTICABILITY OF THE RESUMPTION OF CASH PAYMENTS in the present state of things, founded on some of the principles of the Bullion Report.
By W. C. 1819.

"The worst evil would be an insufficient currency, let "that currency be of what it may."

A VIEW OF OUR LATE AND OF OUR FUTURE CURRENCY.
Walter Hall. 1819.

1819

A LETTER ADDRESSED TO THE RT. HON. ROBT. PEEL, Late Chairman of the Committee of Secrecy appointed to consider of the State of the B. of E., with reference to the expediency of the resumption of Cash Payments at the period fixed by law.
Samuel Turner, F.R.S.   1819.

Insists that £1 and £2 Notes drove the Gold Coin out of circulation, and would begin resumption of Cash payments by calling them in. Speaks highly of the Bank.

THE REAL CAUSE OF THE HIGH PRICE OF BULLION.
1819.

Attributes the rise of prices generally, and of "Bullion "in particular, ... by no means solely to an excess of "paper circulation, ... but to the great increase of "Taxation."

A LETTER TO THE RT. HON. EARL OF LIVERPOOL ON THE IMPOSSIBILITY OF A SPEEDY RETURN TO A GOLD CURRENCY.
C. Lyne.   1819.

Rather above the average of the tracts in favour of the continuance of restriction.

THREE LETTERS ON THE CAUSES OF THE PRESENT STATE OF THE EXCHANGES AND PRICE OF GOLD BULLION, as printed in the *Times* under the signature of "An Old Merchant," with an introductory Address by the Earl of Lauderdale.
1819.

Contends that the high price of Bullion was not owing to over-issue of paper, but to the fact that the Mint regulations, "recently changed," made it pay to export Gold and to import Silver. In England the Mint relative values between the two metals were as 1 to $14\frac{16}{100}$, "at the "time when the Mint proportions in France were fixed at "1 to $15\frac{1}{2}$."

1819

A Protest entered in the Journals of the House of Lords against the second reading of a Bill, entitled — An Act to continue the Restrictions on Cash Payments by the B. of E. until 1st May, 1823, and to provide for the gradual resumption, &c., and to permit the Exportation of Gold, &c.
 By the Earl of Lauderdale.   1819.

 Follows the same line of argument as the "Old " Merchant" (*v. s.*)

Elementary Propositions illustrative of the Principles of Currency.
 Henry Drummond.   1819.

Specimens and Description of Perkins' and Fairman's Siderographic Plan to Prevent Forgery, being the Reports as made to the Commissioners for preventing the Forgery of Bank Notes.   1819.

 The "description" is composed mostly of letters and extracts from reports read before the Commissioners by J. C. Dyer, who appears to have had an interest in the invention. The plates are exquisitely engraved, the "geometric lathe" borderings being very fine. It is admitted that portions of the plate could be imitated, and that portions of the plate could be transposed; the design, too, is very complex; these were weak points. The principal press was in Philadelphia, under the superintendence of Perkins. The system had already been adopted by several of the American Banks, and is, now, still in use.

Principles of a more Perfect System of Currency formed in Precious or Non-Intrinsic Metals, &c., or an Intrinsic Self-Gauging Coin, &c. (With Plates.)
 Sir Wm. Congreve, Bart.   1819.

 An ingenious, but scarcely practical, idea.

1820—1822

A THEORETIC DISCOURSE ON THE NATURE AND PROPERTY OF MONEY, canvassing particularly the notion respecting its dependency on the Precious Metals, in which its abstract quality is likewise considered according to its relations with Foreign Exchanges, containing a few strictures on a prevalent mode of treating such subjects and others, and concluding with some observations on the connection between the B. of E. and Government.

    Ephraim Gompertz.   1820.

LETTERS ADDRESSED TO THE RIGHT HON. THE EARL OF LIVERPOOL, AND THE RIGHT HON. NICHOLAS VANSITTART.   1820.

ELEMENTARY THOUGHTS ON THE BULLION QUESTION, THE NATIONAL DEBT, THE RESOURCES OF GREAT BRITAIN, &c.   Barnstaple, 1820.

    David Ricardo thought highly of this little book.

THE BANK, THE STOCK EXCHANGE, &c.; an Exposé touching their various mysteries from the times of Boyd, the Martyred Goldschmidt, &c., to those of Bowles, Aslett, &c.   1821.

    The style may be judged from the names given to typical characters, such as Overreach, Doubleface, Generous, and others, who figure in the work.

ON PROTECTION TO AGRICULTURE.
    David Ricardo.   1822.

    Appendix A. — Representation of Bank Directors to Chancellor of Exchequer ordered by the House of Commons to be printed 21st May, 1819. Concerns Cash Payments.

1822—1823

REASONS WHY THE BANK OUGHT NOT TO REDUCE THE RATE OF DISCOUNT TO £4 PER CENT., &c., &c.
> By an Impartial Observer. Second Edition.
> 1822.

A LETTER ADDRESSED TO DAVID RICARDO, ESQ., M.P. on the true principle of estimating the extent of the late Depreciation in the Currency, and on the effect of Mr. Peel's Bill for the Resumption of Cash Payments by the Bank.
> Thos. Paget. 1822.

AN ESSAY ON THE GENERAL PRINCIPLES AND PRESENT PRACTICE OF BANKING IN ENGLAND AND SCOTLAND, with observations on the justice and policy of an immediate alteration in the Charter of the B. of E., and the measures to be pursued to effect it.
> Published in Newcastle. 1822.
> (T. Joplin?) see 1826.

Worth reading for its remarks on Bank management, and its comparison of the Scotch and English systems. States that the only district in England where B. of E. Notes were then much circulated was Lancashire. (Lord Liverpool, in his letter to the Bank, in January, 1826, proposing Branch Banks of England, corroborates this fact.) The Author complains of the insecurity of the Private Banks, and proposes the establishment of Joint Stock Banks, as being more secure, and the repeal of VI. Anne, cap. 22, "No more than six persons, &c."

EQUITABLE ADJUSTMENT. SPEECH OF THE RT. HON. W. HUSKISSON in the House of Commons, 11th June, 1822, on Mr. Western's motion concerning the resumption of Cash Payments.
> 1823.

1823

OBSERVATIONS ON THE SPEECH OF THE RT. HON. W. HUSKISSON, &c., &c.
C. C. Western, M.P.   1823.

Western moved for a Committee to consider the effects of Act 59 Geo. III. Cap. 49, which provided for the gradual return to Cash payments.

Huskisson strongly opposed any tampering with the Standard, and pointed out that the right thing, viz., the resumption of Cash payments, must necessarily involve a certain amount of distress, and compared the situation in 1822 to that in 1696. Western, however, could not see the parallel.

The strength of Huskisson's position is shown by the annoyance of his opponent at the title *Equitable* Adjustment, Western proclaiming that he shall say nothing on the point of pecuniary adjustment of contract, &c.

ORIGIN OF PAPER MONEY. J. Klaproth. 1823.

FACTS RELATIVE TO THE B. OF E., explaining the Nature and Influence of the Bank Charter, with a view of the causes and consequences of the suspension and restoration of the use of Standard Coin. (1823?)

A thoroughly practical piece of writing, full of facts, with valuable reprints of correspondence between the Government and the Bank.

THE BANE AND ANTIDOTE, &c., &c.
S. Rogers.   1823.

Proposes to raise the price of Gold to £8 per oz., and says: "It would electrify the people of all nations."

No doubt of it, especially the first nation that might adopt the suggestion.

1824—1825

PLAN FOR THE ESTABLISHMENT OF A NATIONAL BANK.
D. Ricardo. (Posthumous.) 1824.

The present system of separation of Issue and Banking Departments nullifies any really important reason herein advocated for a National Bank. How the National Bank Notes were to get into circulation except by the deposit of Bullion in exchange is not made quite clear.

PIERCE EGAN'S ACCOUNT OF THE TRIAL OF MR. FAUNTLEROY FOR FORGERY at the Sessions House in the Old Bailey, on Saturday, the 30th October, 1824, before Mr. Justice Park and Mr. Baron Garrow. 1824.

Fauntleroy was a partner in the Bank of Marsh & Co. He forged the signatures to many Powers of Attorney for the Sale of Stock for eight years before discovery.

There was produced at the trial a paper in his own handwriting giving details of the forgeries, and stating that he had committed them to obtain sufficient money to keep up the credit of his firm, and without the knowledge of his partners. That the Bank had injured his house by refusing to take its acceptances, and that "they should smart for it." They did; the total loss was £360,000. In this man, one of those last hanged for forgery, good and evil were mixed to a far greater degree than usual, his character being a remarkable psychical study.

The Appendix enumerates eighteen capital offences in respect to the Stocks.

AN ILLUSTRATION OF MR. JOPLIN'S VIEWS ON CURRENCY AND A PLAN FOR ITS IMPROVEMENT, together with applications to the present state of the Money Market, in a series of Letters.
By an Economist. 1825.

Reprinted from the *Courier*, with an Appendix.

1825—1826

AN ESSAY ON THE MANAGEMENT & MISMANAGEMENT OF THE CURRENCY.

By the Author of an Essay on the Rent of Land.　　　　　　　　　　1825.

CAUSES OF THE PRESENT DEPRESSION IN THE MONEY MARKET, with a suggestion for its relief.

John Exeter.　　　　　　　　　1825.

Proposes to establish an Exchequer Bank to work the Exchequer Bills.

AN ESSAY ON THE GENERAL PRINCIPLES AND PRESENT PRACTICE OF BANKING IN ENGLAND AND SCOTLAND, &c., &c. Fifth Edition.

T. Joplin (*see* 1822).　　　　　　1826.

AN ATTEMPT TO EXPLAIN FROM FACTS THE EFFECTS OF THE ISSUES OF THE B. OF E. UPON ITS OWN INTERESTS, PUBLIC CREDIT, AND COUNTRY BANKS.

R. Mushet.　　　　　　　　　1826.

Amongst other things, he proposes "an extension of the "metallic basis of the currency, and that no Notes should "be in circulation under £20." He also looks forward to the establishment of the Joint Stock system as beneficial alike to the public and the B. of E.

Appendix giving prices of Gold, Silver, £3 per cent. Consols, and course of Exchange with Hamburg and Paris from 1815 to 1825:—

	HIGHEST.		LOWEST.
Gold, ℔ oz.,	£5 : 7s., 4th April, 1815.	£3 : 17s. 6d.,	2nd July, 1822.
Consols, %,	96¼, 4th May, 1824.	56¾,	1st Sept., 1815.

On 30th December, 1825, Consols stood at 81.

On 30th August, 1825, Bar Gold was quoted at £3 : 17s. 10½d. ℔ oz.

1826

A LETTER TO THE EDITOR OF THE EDINBURGH WEEKLY JOURNAL from Malachi Malagrowther, Esquire (*i.e.* Sir Walter Scott), on the Proposed Change of Currency as they affect, or are intended to affect, the Kingdom of Scotland.

Third Edition. 1826.

A SECOND LETTER, ditto, Second Edition. **1826.**

A THIRD LETTER, ditto, Second Edition. **1826.**

Scott himself, in his diary, mentions writing them (*see* Lockhart's Life). At the time of their appearance, too, he speaks of them in a letter to Dundas Croker; in fact, their authorship seems to have been an open secret. They deal with the suppression of the "Small Note" circulation, and were referred to by the Chancellor of the Exchequer, on opening the Budget, 19th March, 1826, as "the incantations "of the First Magician of the age." Full of wisdom and wit.

REMARKS ON THE BANK RESTRICTION ACT AND THE SINKING FUND.

Isaac L. Goldsmid.   1826.

CONSIDERATIONS ON THE STATE OF THE CURRENCY.

T. Tooke, F.R.S.   1826.

The work was at first meant as a sequel to the first part of the "High and Low Prices," published 1822, but he afterwards devoted it more especially to the consideration of the events between that date and 1826.

He argues that the Bank ought to have unloaded, at any rate the greater part of, the "Dead Weight Annuity" as soon as the increased issues for payment upon the purchases produced a bad effect on the exchanges, or to have raised the rate as a means of decreasing the redundant issue. Also that the non-publication of the Bank's accounts introduced too large an element of uncertainty, and suggests the obvious remedy.

1826

The greatest evils, however, were the precarious state of the country issues. "Every country Banker ought to "be called upon to give some pledge of his ability to pay "on demand the Notes which he may be permitted to "issue." Further, "there is one part of that circulation "which ought not upon any footing or with any modification "to be any longer tolerated. I mean the Notes under £5."

Some Country Banks grumbled if the public asked for gold; he rightly says: "If there is any feeling of the "harshness of demanding coin for the Notes of a Bank, "such Notes are more or less imperfectly convertible."

THE PRESENT CRITICAL STATE OF THE COUNTRY DEVELOPED, or an exhibition of the true causes of the calamitous derangement of the Banking and Commercial System, shewing the essential distinction between the solidity of the National B. of E. and that of the Country Banks.
By an Individual. 1826.

Has much useful information concerning the relations between the Bank and the Government from 1795 to 1826.

THE B. OF E. DEFENDED, OR THE PRINCIPAL CAUSE OF THE HIGH PRICES DEMONSTRATED, &c., &c.
By Verax. 1826.

A tract in advance of its times, advocating Bimetallism and a monopoly of Issue for the Bank.

AN ENQUIRY INTO THE ORIGIN AND INCREASE OF THE PAPER CURRENCY OF THE KINGDOM.
1826.

THE STATE OF OUR CIRCULATION AND CURRENCY BRIEFLY CONSIDERED, in a Letter to a Friend.
1826.

1826—1828

THE STATE OF THE CIRCULATION AND CURRENCY BRIEFLY CONSIDERED, in a Second Letter to a Friend, with an Appendix (*v.s.*)

Jasper Atkinson. 1826.

OBSERVATIONS ON PAPER MONEY, BANKING AND OVERTRADING, including those parts of the evidence taken before the House of Commons which explain the Scotch System of Banking.

Sir Hy. Parnell, Bart., M.P. 1827.

In Section VII., on the B. of E., he argues that the privileges of the B. of E. were too exclusive, and liable to abuse, but would give full compensation for any loss the Bank would sustain by surrendering them. Good paragraphs on Scotch and Irish banking.

AN ADDRESS TO THE PROPRIETORS OF BANK STOCK, THE LONDON AND COUNTRY BANKERS, AND THE PUBLIC IN GENERAL, ON THE AFFAIRS OF THE B. OF E. 1828.

Abuses the Bank, and demands periodical publication of its accounts in the *Gazette*. An appendix of 80 pages of Extracts, &c.

A VIEW OF THE MONEY SYSTEM OF ENGLAND FROM THE CONQUEST, with proposals for establishing a secure and equable Currency.

James Taylor. 1828.

Proposes B. of E. Notes as legal tender for all payments of £1 and upwards, and the Bank to pay their Notes in coin on demand at the market price.

1829—1830

THE CASE OF THE CURRENCY, WITH ITS REMEDY.

By Richard Moore. 1829.

The "Remedy" was "a sterling standard Imperial Mint "paper Note," and all Issuing Bankers to deposit security to the amount of their Issue with the Government. This deposit system is now in operation in the United States.

A LETTER TO LORD GRENVILLE on the effects ascribed to the resumption of Cash Payments on the value of the Currency.

Thos. Tooke. 1829.

Contends that the contraction of the Currency was not produced by Peel's Bill, or by the Bank's preparation for Cash payments.

Appendix with Statistics, &c., and A Second Letter, ditto, ditto, "endeavouring to prove the same proposition "by a different process."

THOUGHTS ON CURRENCY AND THE MEANS OF PROMOTING NATIONAL PROSPERITY by the adoption of "An Improved Circulation," founded on the security of Solid Property, &c., &c., &c.

Rt. Hon. Sir Jno. Sinclair, Bart. 1829.

ON CREDIT CURRENCY AND ITS SUPERIORITY TO COIN, in support of a Petition for the Establishment of a Cheap, Safe, and Sufficient Circulating Medium.

G. Poulett Scrope. 1830.

1830

A Letter to the Duke of Wellington on the Currency.

James Taylor.   1830.

In support of his proposals in his tract published in 1828 (*v. s.*)

Three Lectures on the Cost of obtaining Money, and on some effects of Private and Government Paper Money.

Nassau W. Senior.   1830.

Testifies to the honesty of the Bank during the period of "Restriction," and compares the enormous depreciation of foreign state paper currency with the relatively slight depreciation of our own, *e.g.*,

Russia   in 1814,   4 Roubles paper = 1 Silver.
Denmark ,, 1813, 1600 Dollars   ,,   = 1   ,,
Austria ,, 1810,   13 Florins   ,,   = 1   ,,

For instance, in Denmark, an article worth six dollars in silver coin, was worth nine thousand six hundred dollars in paper money, and so on.

Remarks on the Question of again permitting the Issue of £1 Notes by the B. of E. and also by Country Banks.   1830.

The question is well stated and the summing-up is against the issue of £1 Notes.

The Principle and Operation of Gold and Silver in Coin, of Paper in Currency, and of Gold and Silver in Buying and Selling, Stated, &c.

Alexander Mundell.   1830.

1831

HISTORICAL SKETCH OF THE B. OF E., with an Examination of the Question as to the Prolongation of the Exclusive Privileges of that Establishment. 8vo., 77 pages. 1831.

J. R. McCulloch published this tract anonymously, but in his "Handbook to Literature of Political Economy" puts his own name to it. Though more of the nature of a compilation, or rather a review, its 77 pages contain more useful and soundly written matter on the subject than any other book before published. His suggestion as to the form in which the weekly accounts should be published has been adopted entirely in principle, and in many of the details.

In speaking of Country Banks of Issue, he says: "It is absolutely imperative upon Government to interfere, "to protect the interest of those who cannot protect them- "selves, either by compelling all individuals applying for "stamps for notes, to give security for their payment, or by "making sure in some other way that they have the means "of paying them, and that the circulation of the notes will "be a benefit and not an injury to the public. A security "of this sort has been exacted in the case of the B. of E., "and the whole" (at that time) "£14,686,000, lent by the "Bank to Government, must be sacrificed before the holders "of her notes can sustain the smallest loss. Her stability "has, therefore, been truly said, by Dr. Smith, to be equal "to that of the British Government."

The five chapters of the book deal with: (1) Convertibility of Bank paper; (2) Historical Sketch of the B. of E.; (3) The B. of E. in connection with the Government and the Public; (4) Prolongation of the Bank Charter; and (5) Appendix.

In a masterly manner he shows in what a false position a "National Bank" (*i.e.*, a Bank conducted by the Government with their own officials), as proposed by Ricardo and others, would stand. He estimates the cost of a convenient site, in the commercial centre, requisite for such a building at £2,000,000. Asks how Government officials could be familiar with the mysteries of the market, pointing out the disadvantage they would be at in comparison with the Bank Directors, men experienced in business. Neither could a National Bank engage in discounting, &c., without

1831—1832

incurring at times the gravest suspicions. He contrasts the independent position of the Bank with that of a mere Government office at the mercy of any party in power. Takes exception to Sir H. Parnell's views on free Banking trade in London, and gives instances of the honesty and great use of the Bank to the nation.

The tabular statement of renewals of the Charter, and Advances to Government, is most clear. Useful Appendix. From 1797-1829 there were 618 capital convictions for forgery of Bank Notes and Post Bills.

A PLAIN STATEMENT OF THE POWER OF THE B. OF E., AND THE USE IT HAS MADE OF IT; with a refutation of the objections made to the Scotch System of Banking, and a reply to the "Historical Sketch of the B. of E." (*q.v.s.*)
    Sir Hy. Parnell.   1832.

SUPPLEMENT TO AN EXAMINATION OF THE EVIDENCE TAKEN BEFORE THE COMMITTEE OF SECRECY ON THE BANK CHARTER.
    A. Mundell.   1832.

Twenty-four pages of (personal?) hostility to the Bank.

LIFE AND ADVENTURES OF THE OLD LADY OF THREADNEEDLE STREET, containing an account of her numerous intrigues with various eminent Statesmen of the past and present times.
    Written by herself.   1832.

Not sufficiently smart for satire, and too slovenly for history.

AN ADDRESS TO THE PROPRIETORS OF BANK STOCK ON THE SUBJECT OF THE CHARTER, THE EXCLUSIVE PRIVILEGE OF BANKING, AND AN INCREASE OF DIVIDEND.
    By J. P. Winter, a Proprietor.   1832.

1832—1833

A Legal Statement of the Real Position of the Government with Relation to the B. of E.

Samuel Wells. Second Edition. 1832.

Rather a well-written tract; criticises the Bank very sharply. Useful appendix of Acts relating to the Bank.

The Evidence that would have been given by Mr. ——— (*i.e.* John Cazenove*), late a Continental Merchant, before the Committee of Secrecy appointed to enquire into the expediency of renewing the Bank Charter. 1832.

Any man by questioning and answering himself can prove his case to his own fancy. Cazenove forgets that had he been sharply cross-examined before the Commission his evidence would probably have been quite different. "Question 71.—Do you conceive the institution of Joint "Stock Banks would be desirable in London? I see no "use in them (!), as the circulation, when properly regulated, "is always as full as it should be; for any Note of any "such Joint Stock Co. a Bank Note of similar amount "must be withdrawn," &c., &c. If he refers only to Banks of Issue he should say so. A very amusing book.

* (British Museum Catalogue.)

A Copy of the Correspondence between the Chancellor of the Exchequer and the B. of E. relative to the Renewal of the Charter. April, 1833.

Chancellor of Exchequer, Lord Althorp.

Governor, B. of E., Mr. J. Horsley Palmer.

Deputy-Governor, Mr. R. M. Raikes.

1833

A DIGEST OF THE EVIDENCE ON THE BANK CHARTER TAKEN BEFORE THE COMMITTEE OF 1832, arranged together with the "Tables" under proper heads. To which are prefixed Strictures and Illustrative Remarks, also copious Indices, &c.
1833.

Inferior to the next work, by Quin, the indices being badly arranged. The remarks are contrary to the tendency of the "Report."

THE TRADE OF BANKING IN ENGLAND, embracing the substance of the evidence taken before the Secret Committee of the House of Commons, digested and arranged under appropriate heads, together with a Summary of the Law applicable to the B. of E., to Private Banks of Issue and Joint Stock Trading Companies.

M. J. Quin. 1833.

With an appendix of statistics and general information. A well-arranged, thoroughly reliable book, with a good index.

STRICTURES ON THE EVIDENCE TAKEN BEFORE THE COMMITTEE OF SECRECY OF THE HOUSE OF COMMONS ON THE B. OF E. CHARTER.

By Scotus. 1833.

Dissatisfied both with the evidence and the Report.

A LETTER TO THE EDITOR OF THE *Times* ON THE QUESTION OF THE BANK CHARTER, shewing the inconsistency of some of the accounts lately furnished by the Bank to the Committee of the House of Commons. 1833.

1833—1836

CURRENCY FALLACIES REFUTED AND PAPER MONEY VINDICATED.
(By Jno. Taylor?) 1833.

IMPORTANT NOTICES OF THAT WHICH CONCERNS THE PECUNIARY CREDIT OF A STATE, AND IN PARTICULAR THAT OF ENGLAND.
Richard Moore. 1833.

Advocates "Mint paper coin co-current with our Gold Money."

THE REVENUE AND EXPENDITURE OF THE UNITED KINGDOM.
Samuel Wells, Barrister. 1834.

Chapters on the Bank and kindred subjects from an extreme point of view; the book, however, is useful for its many quotations of Acts and dates. Abuses the Bank as one of the chief bloodsuckers of the national vitals, &c., &c.

LETTERS ON THE B. OF E., with a Prospectus of a new Joint Stock Banking Company.
By a Liverpool Merchant. 1836.

These letters were addressed to the Editor of *The Albion*. Advises the Bankers to form "a United Banks of England," as it is "more easy to construct new than to mend old institutions."

The new one was, of course, to have all the advantages and none of the defects of the B. of E., which he considers past praying for.

A REVIEW OF THE TRADE OF BANKING IN ENGLAND AND IRELAND, &c., also a Summary of the Evidence taken before the Secret Committee of Joint Stock Banks during the last Session of Parliament.
Richard Gordon. 1836.

1837

THE CAUSES AND CONSEQUENCES OF THE PRESSURE ON THE MONEY MARKET, with a Statement of the Action of the B. of E., from 1st October, 1833, to 27th December, 1836.

J. Horsley Palmer (a Bank Director, 1811–56).

1837.

An able defence of the Bank's line of action during the period above-mentioned. Shows that the drain of Bullion was due to the negotiation of numerous foreign Loans, the change in the U. S. Mint regulations, and to the increase in the number of Joint Stock Banks, and to their excessive issue; these circumstances together forming a counteracting influence to the Bank's action.

The appendix contains the correspondence which took place in 1826 between the Treasury (Lord Liverpool) and the Bank, with respect to the establishment of Branch Banks of England.

This and the following tract are most valuable, and cast a clear light on the financial history of the period.

REFLECTIONS SUGGESTED BY A PERUSAL OF MR. J. HORSLEY PALMER'S PAMPHLET ON THE CAUSES AND CONSEQUENCES OF THE PRESSURE ON THE MONEY MARKET.

S. Jones Loyd (Lord Overstone). 1837.

Thinks the state of the case in Mr. Horsley Palmer's tract is "not proven."

Advocates the separation of the Banking and Issue Departments and an extension of the central issuer's monopoly so as to give her more control over the subordinate issuers.

"The one simple duty which the manager of the "Currency has to perform is that of making the amount "of the paper circulation vary precisely as the amount of "the circulation would have varied had it been exclusively "metallic."

1837

"A Bank of Issue is entrusted with the creation of the "circulating medium.

"A Bank of Deposit and Discount is concerned only "with the use, distribution, or application of the circulating "medium."

Further Reflections on the State of the Currency and the Action of the B. of E.

S. Jones Loyd (Lord Overstone).

23rd December, 1837.

The object of this treatise was to lay further emphasis on the chief points in the "Reflections, &c.," especially "the essential difference between a Bank of Issue and a "Bank of Deposit and Discount," and to practically illustrate the correctness of his views by reference to the proceedings of the B. of E. during the financial pressure which had occurred since the date of his first publication.

The Cause of the Present Money Crisis Explained, in answer to the Pamphlet of Mr. J. Horsley Palmer, and a remedy pointed out by W. Bennison. Second Edition. 1837.

He blames the B. of E. and thinks Mr. Horsley Palmer laid too much stress on the careless management of the country Banks.

"It may be said, the applications for discount are so "pressing that it would instantly bring on a panic if these "demands were not complied with, and thus the Bank is "compelled *reluctantly* to increase her securities. This I "believe to be actually the case; nevertheless, she ought "at the same time to diminish the amount by the sale of "such securities as cannot be forced back upon her. If "she persevered steadily diminishing the *total amount* of "securities gradually to the extent of only half a million "a month, while she discounted all good bills offered to "her, a very few months would bring us into smooth "water again."

1837—1838

A WORD ON THE BANK AND PAPER SYSTEM OF ENGLAND. 1837.

THOUGHTS ON THE PRINCIPLES OF BANKS AND THE WISDOM OF LEGISLATIVE INTERFERENCE. 1837.

OBSERVATIONS ON THE CRISIS 1836–37, with Suggestions for a Remedy against Commercial Pressures.
 By a Merchant. 1837.

A LETTER TO THE RT. HON. LORD VISCOUNT MELBOURNE ON THE CAUSES OF THE RECENT DERANGEMENT IN THE MONEY MARKET, AND ON BANK REFORM.
 R. Torrens, F.R.S. 1837.

 Insists that the Circulation should be allowed to contract or expand according to the state of the foreign exchanges, and that separation of the Issue and Banking Departments is necessary.

OBSERVATIONS ON THE SYSTEM OF METALLIC CURRENCY ADOPTED (*sic*) TO THIS COUNTRY.
 W. H. Morrison. Second Edition. 1837.

 Bimetallist, advocating "a double circulation of Gold "and Silver free from the restraints imposed by our present "system."

ARTICLES ON BANKING AND CURRENCY, from the *Economist* newspaper.
 T. Joplin. 1838.

1838

REMARKS ON SOME PREVALENT ERRORS WITH RESPECT TO CURRENCY AND BANKING, and Suggestions to the Legislature and the Public as to the Improvement in the Monetary System.
Geo. Warde Norman.   1838.

In this tract, which did good work in its time, the author, a Bank Director, 1821-70, points out, (1) the dissimilarity of the functions of a Bank of Issue and an ordinary Banking concern, (2) that while ordinary Banking trade should be perfectly free, it is far better for the issue of Notes to be a monopoly, for the sake both of the Banking world and of the general public.

He proposes an Issue based one-third on coin and bullion and two-thirds on "profitable securities, the discharge of "public debts." After insisting on the rate of Exchange as the real criterion of the state of the currency, he says, with regard to a monopoly of Issue: "The managers of one "issuing establishment, supposing all their proceedings to "be made public, would be placed under a feeling of "responsibility which would render it almost impossible for "them to forget this great truth, but supposing instead of "one that we have ten or a hundred Banks, the responsibility "is so divided as to become inefficient.

"The business of Issue, well conducted, can yield but "a moderate profit, but if ill conducted so far as the public "is concerned, it may yield a far more considerable profit— "can any reasonable man doubt which course would be "pursued? The loss and inconvenience of over-issues do not "always fall upon the peccant bank, but on its neighbours."

Gives a resumé of Torrens' plan for the separation of the two departments, which provided that the "circulation" department should strictly confine itself to the exchange of Gold for Notes and Notes for Gold with the following exceptions:—(1) Liberty to buy or sell silver up to £2,000,000 or £3,000,000. (2) It should be compulsory at all times to buy bar or foreign gold at 77s. 6d. per oz., and be allowed to sell at 77s. 9d. per oz. (3) Permission to lend Notes on Coin or Bullion at a low rate of Interest, say, £1 per cent., so as to afford facilities to commerce, whilst leading to no derangement of currency, and that complete publicity should exist. The remaining provisions were mostly matters of detail.

1838—1840

The writer agrees to a great extent with the Torrens plan, of which many suggestions were embodied in the 1844 Act. After setting forth the whole of the matter most clearly, he says in conclusion : "However desirous "the Directors of the B. of E. might be to introduce the "proposed system, they cannot be expected to do so on "their own responsibility, especially in the existing state "of public opinion, which has almost everything to learn "on the subject of currency."

This was, unfortunately, only too true, notwithstanding the severe lessons of the Restriction, and the repeated panics and failures among the country issuers. In spite of the light thrown on the subject by the 1810 Bullion Report, and the labours of Ricardo, McCulloch, Blake, and Huskisson, the public, and, curiously enough, the financial section of it especially, were still all at sea, blown hither and thither with "winds of doctrine," and had it not been for the work of a very few men like Horsley Palmer, Jones Loyd, Warde Norman, and Torrens, who were luckily both capable and of sound views, and influential not only in the "money "world" but outside it, the whole financial system might have suffered.

CAUSES WHICH LEAD TO A BANK RESTRICTION BILL.

Henry Drummond.   1839.

ON MONEY DERANGEMENTS, in a Letter addressed to the Proprietors of Bank Stock.

Wm. Ward.   1840.

He is "under the influence of the warmest feelings in "the welfare of one of the most useful and creditable "institutions that ever yet existed, &c.," but "he wishes "to see removed one of the greatest injuries the country "ever encountered, viz., a paper circulation not regulated "by any determinate reference to a metallic standard of "value."

1810—1842

REFLECTIONS ON THE CURRENCY. By a Yorkshire Manufacturer. 1840.

REMARKS ON THE MANAGEMENT OF THE CIRCULATION, and on the Condition and Conduct of the B. of E., and of the Country Issuers during the year 1839.

    S. Jones Loyd (Lord Overstone). 1840.

Establishes the position taken up in his "Reflections, &c." 1837 (q. v.), and would give the Bank greater control over the Country Bankers, who usually restricted their accommodation when too late.

CURRENCY AND BANKING. A Review of some of the Principles and Plans that have recently engaged public attention with reference to the Administration of the Currency.

    J. W. Gilbart (of the London & Westminster Bank). 1841.

THE SYSTEM OF THE LONDON BANKERS' CLEARANCES, and their effect upon the Currency explained and exemplified by Formulæ of the Clearing House Accounts.

    W. Tate (Author of "The Modern Cambist"). 1841.

THOUGHTS ON THE CURRENCY. 1842.

METALLIC, PAPER, AND CREDIT, CURRENCY, and the means of regulating their quantity and value.

    J. W. Bosanquet. 1842.

Holds "that when the currency is not in itself unsound "from excessive issue, the principle of convertibility may "be suspended in cases of emergency without danger to "the value of the currency," and that the enforcement of the principle of convertibility may at times be wrong.

1843—1844

CURRENCY AND THE COUNTRY. J. G. Hubbard (since, Lord Addington). 1843.

McCulloch mentions this as "A valuable tract in favour "of a single Bank of Issue." The Author was a Director of the Bank from 1838—1889.

BANKS AND BANKERS.
Daniel Hardcastle, junior (*i. e.* R. Page).
Second Edition. 1843.

Racily written, full of anecdotal interest, and at times very extreme in the views advocated. He is, doubtless, however, quite right in saying that the same amount of information could not, then, be found in one extant volume.

Well worth reading.

SPEECH OF BENJAMIN HAWES, ESQ., in Opposition to the Second Reading of the B. of E. Charter Bill, 13th June, 1844.

TWO LETTERS TO THE RT. HON. SIR ROBT. PEEL ON HIS PROPOSED BANKING MEASURES. BY AN EX-M.P. 1844.

Foretells all sorts of catastrophes in case the Charter Act were passed. The pamphlet was probably by a country Banker.

REMARKS ON THE EXPEDIENCY OF RESTRICTING THE ISSUE OF PROMISSORY NOTES TO A SINGLE ISSUING BODY.
Sir Wm. Clay, Bt., M.P. 1844.

SPEECHES OF THE RT. HON. SIR ROBT. PEEL, BT., in the House of Commons, 6th and 20th May, 1844, on the Renewal of the Bank Charter and the state of the Law respecting Currency and Banking. 1844.

1844—1847

SPEECH OF CHAS. WOOD, ESQ., in the Debate on Sir R. Peel's Resolutions on Banking, Monday, 20th May. 1844.

ON THE REGULATION OF CURRENCIES AND THE WORKING OF THE NEW BANK CHARTER ACT.
Jno. Fullarton. 1844.

THOUGHTS ON THE SEPARATION OF THE DEPARTMENTS OF THE B. OF E.
S. Jones Loyd (Lord Overstone). 1844.

THE LITERATURE OF POLITICAL ECONOMY.
J. R. McCulloch. 1845.

It is described on the title-page as a "Classified Catalogue "of select publications in the different departments of that "Science, with Historical, Critical, and Biographical Notices."

An indispensable book to all students of the subject.

WORKS OF DAVID RICARDO, ESQ., M.P., with a Notice of the Life and Writings of the Author.
By J. R. McCulloch. 1846.

This edition, which has a good index, includes the "Essay on the Funding System," written for the Supplement to the Sixth Edition of the Encyclopædia Britannica.

McCulloch was an ideal Editor for Ricardo.

ON THE OPERATION OF THE BANK CHARTER ACT OF 1844 AS IT AFFECTS COMMERCIAL CREDIT.
By R. Torrens. 1847.

Insists that the Act entirely fulfilled its purposes.

1847

THE B. OF E. JUSTIFIED IN THEIR PRESENT COURSE.

By Jas. Ward. 1847.

Against the 1844 Act. Contends the Bank was right to discount liberally to help the market.

THE PETITION OF THE MERCHANTS, BANKERS AND TRADERS OF LONDON, AGAINST THE BANK CHARTER ACT, with Comments on each Clause.
1847.

LETTER TO THE RT. HON. SIR CHARLES WOOD, BART., M.P., Chancellor of the Exchequer, on the Monetary Pressure and Commercial Distress of 1847.

By Jno. Gellibrand Hubbard (afterwards Lord Addington). 1847.

A FINANCIAL, MONETARY, AND STATISTICAL HISTORY OF ENGLAND, FROM 1688 TO THE PRESENT TIME, derived principally from Official Documents. In seventeen Letters addressed to the young men of Great Britain.

Thos. Doubleday. 1847.

This pessimistic effusion of over 400 pages must have taken some time to write, and contains evidence that its author possessed a certain amount of culture, and, unfortunately, many prejudices as well. The Bank Act of 1844, the Railway Constructors, in fact, all, was wrong, quite wrong; the destruction of all commerce and finance was at hand, and for this final catastrophe the Bank Act was more to blame than anything else. He had better have stuck to facts. It is curious that in speaking of the Bank Restriction Act, which excites his boundless hatred, he quotes Gilbart's evidence before a Committee—"That "the Act was not only a necessity, but good policy."

1847—1849

The concluding passage calls to mind Artemus Ward's maxim, viz., "It isn't safe to prophesy unless you know." "It is quite within the verge of possibility that as the "scorpion when surrounded by fire is said to sting itself "to death, so the Bank Act of Peel may, by force of "circumstances, be made to bring down the very fabric it "was made to protect, a consummation of which the "poetical would not be less conspicuous than the abstract "and final justice."

A Review of the Practical Working of the Act of 1844 for Regulating the Issue of Notes by the B. of E.

J. W. Gilbart, F.R.S. 1849.

History of the B. of E., its Times and Traditions.

John Francis. Third Edition. (1849?)

A most excellent work, graphically written and thoroughly reliable.

A contemporary number of the *Economist* says:—"Mr. Francis has made a subject that is, generally, "repulsively dry, a matter of light reading. Instead of "long rows of figures he gives us curious and interesting "stories, ... and his book will be more extensively read "than a mere political economical history." The appendix contains a reprint of Godfrey's Tract, "A Short Account "of the B. of E.," a copy of the correspondence between the Chancellor of the Exchequer and the B. of E. relative to the renewal of the Charter of 1844, a List of Directors from 1694 to 1847, and a few pages of statistics.

Mr. Francis was a clerk in the B. of E., and subsequently filled the important post of Accountant-General to the Bank.

1850—1853

THE HISTORY OF BANKING, with a comprehensive account of the Origin, Rise and Progress of the Banks of England, Ireland and Scotland.

    Wm. Jno. Lawson.   1850.

A capital book, by an interesting writer. Always chatty and anecdotal throughout, yet the amount of solid information given in the work is enormous. A second Edition appeared in 1855.

THE CITY, OR THE PHYSIOLOGY OF LONDON BUSINESS, WITH SKETCHES ON 'CHANGE, &c.
        1852.

Chatty notes on City men and manners, not forgetting the Bank.

A LETTER TO THOS. BARING, ESQ. ON THE EFFECTS OF THE CALIFORNIAN AND AUSTRALIAN GOLD DISCOVERIES.

    Frederick Scheer.   1852.

SOME OBSERVATIONS ON THE RECENT SUPPLIES OF GOLD, with Remarks on Mr. Scheer's Letter to Sir T. Baring.

    Andrew Johnson, of the Bullion Office, B. of E.
        1852.

REMARKS ON THE PRODUCTION OF THE PRECIOUS METALS AND ON THE DEPRECIATION OF GOLD.

    By M. Chevalier. (Translated from the French by D. Forbes Campbell.)   1853.

Includes Letter to the Governor of B. of E. (Thomson Hankey, Esq.), and a useful appendix, with tables, &c.

1855—1856

Bank of England Barometer for 1855. 1855.

Gives rules for the "prognosticatory" interpretation of the weekly published returns. If "pecuniary assets" of the Bank stand below £24,000,000 the barometric indication may be considered as "stormy," if above that amount, "set fair."

By "pecuniary assets" he means Gold in the Issue Department and Notes and Coin in the Banking Department.

On the Security and Manufacture of Bank Notes. A Lecture delivered at the Royal Institution.

Henry Bradbury.   9th May, 1856.

Describes the different methods of engraving Notes, and pleads for better Art in their design. One of the illustrations of specimen Notes, designed by John Leighton, is splendidly engraved.

The Financier Law, His Scheme and Times.

P. A. Cochut.   1856.

A graphic account of the Origin, Maturity and Wreck of the Mississippi Scheme.

After the great catastrophe the following "affiche" was posted on the walls in Paris :—

> " Beelzebub begat Law,
> " Law begat the Mississippi,
> " The Mississippi begat the Scheme,
> " The Scheme begat the Paper,
> " The Paper begat the Bank,
> " The Bank begat the Note,
> " The Note begat the Share,
> " The Share begat the Stockjobbing,
> " The Stockjobbing begat the Registration,
> " The Registration begat the Account,
> " The Account begat the general Balance,
> " The Balance begat Zero,
> " From which power of begetting was taken away."

A concise and not inaccurate description.

1857

A Brief Historical Relation of State Affairs from September, 1678, to April, 1714.
Narcissus Luttrell.   Oxford, 1857.

Luttrell, who was born in 1657, was a Fellow-Commoner of St. John's College, Cambridge; his degree of M.A. was conferred by Royal Mandate in 1675. He seems to have taken no active part in the events of his time, leading a secluded life at Chelsea, where he died in 1732.

The "Relation" consists of an onlooker's very brief, not to say bald, notes of passing events. The MS., which remained comparatively unknown till Macaulay quoted from it in his History of England, is in the library of All Souls College, Oxford. It was printed in 1857, in six volumes, by the Delegates of the Oxford University Press. It is much to be regretted that, while they were about it, they did not provide the book with a better index, instead of the wretched apology for one it now has. An adequate index would have greatly enhanced the value of so rich a mine of information. Rogers has used the book in his "First Nine Years of B. of E." (*q.v.* 1887). The following extracts, in addition to their intrinsic interest, show the style of the book.

" Thursday, 21st June, 1694. The Commissioners for
" the new Bank came this morning to Mercers' Chapel,
" where the books were opened; the Lords of the Treasury
" came themselves and subscribed £10,000 for the Queen;
" . . . . 'tis said the subscriptions already amount to
" £300,000, such as subscribe before Sunday will be allowed
" 50s. per cent. Rebate, and on Monday 40s., but afterwards
" 'twill fall 5s. per day. Mr. Knight, Treasurer of the
" Customs, and Mr. Burton, of the Exchequer, are impowred
" by the Commissioners to take subscriptions for ease of
" people."

" Saturday, 29th September, 1694. Yesterday a General
" Court of the Members of the B. of E. mett at Mercers'
" Chapell, when the Governor, Sir John Houblon, acquainted
" them there was a necessity for their removing out of
" that place, and, therefore, he had taken Grocers' Hall for
" eleven years, and told them the Bank was in a flourishing
" condition, and that the By-lawes were prepared and laid
" before Serjeant Levinz."

1857

"Saturday, 28th September, 1695. The Bank of England, "not having that successe in their Mint at Antwerp for "coyning Money to pay our army as they expected, "have borrowed £200,000 of the Bank of Amsterdam, "at £4 per cent., the King giving his word at the same "time to see them reimburst, which money they have paid "to His Majesty's Army in Flanders, without remitting "hence."

"14th October, 1695. At Old Bailey Sessions four (men) "were fined considerable summes and stood in the pillory "for cheating the B. of E."

"5th December, 1696. Sir John Houblon, Governor of "the Bank, delivered to House of Parliament the debts and "credits thereof; 'tis said the Bank is worth £280,000, "their debts paid."

SIR ROBERT PEEL'S ACT OF 1844, REGULATING THE ISSUE OF BANK NOTES, VINDICATED.
G. Arbuthnot. 1857.

A SELECT COLLECTION OF SCARCE AND VALUABLE TRACTS, &c., ON PAPER CURRENCY AND BANKING. ("The Overstone Tracts.") 1857.

(*Vide* 1857. National Debt Section.)

(*Copy of Table of Contents.*)

I. A DISCOURSE CONCERNING THE CURRENCIES OF THE BRITISH PLANTATIONS IN AMERICA, especially with regard to their Paper Money, with a P.S. thereto.
Boston, 1740.   Reprinted, London, 1751.

II. BANKS AND PAPER MONEY (from Essays, Moral and Political, &c.)
D. Hume.   1752.

III. ESSAYS ON PAPER MONEY AND BANKING (from Essays on the Public Debt, Frugality, &c.)
By Patrick, fifth Lord Elibank.   1755.

IV. ESSAYS ON BANKS AND PAPER CREDIT (from Characteristics of the Present State of Great Britain). Attributed to Rev. Dr. Robert Wallace.
1758.

V. NOTE ON SUSPENSION OF CASH PAYMENTS AT THE B. OF E. IN 1797.

(J. R. McCulloch.)

VI. THE UTILITY OF COUNTRY BANKS CONSIDERED, &c. 1802? (circ.)

VII. AN ENQUIRY CONCERNING THE PAPER CREDIT OF GREAT BRITAIN.

Henry Thornton. 1802.

VIII. NOTE ON THE STATE OF THE EXCHANGE BETWEEN LONDON AND DUBLIN from 1797 to 1804.

(J. R. McCulloch.)

IX. REMARKS ON THE PAPER CURRENCY.

By Lord Liverpool. From his "Coins of the "Realm." 1805.

X. THE HIGH PRICE OF BULLION A PROOF OF THE DEPRECIATION OF BANK NOTES.

By David Ricardo. Fourth Edition, corrected.
1811.

XI. REPORT FROM SELECT COMMITTEE OF THE HOUSE OF COMMONS ON THE HIGH PRICE OF GOLD BULLION.

Ordered to be printed, 8th June. 1810.

1857

XII. OBSERVATIONS ON THE PRINCIPLES WHICH REGULATE THE COURSE OF EXCHANGE, AND ON THE PRESENT DEPRECIATED STATE OF THE CURRENCY.

By Wm. Blake, F.R.S. 1810.

XIII. THE QUESTION CONCERNING THE DEPRECIATION OF OUR CURRENCY. Stated and Examined by Wm. Huskisson, M.P. Third Edition, corrected.

1819.

Lord Overstone, a notable figure in the financial world of his day, printed, at his own expense, in the "fifties," the above volume, one of a series since known to fame as the "Overstone Tracts." They consist chiefly of reprints of scarce and important works, most difficult of access prior to the issue of this series. Although all are interesting, only those volumes which more particularly bear on the central subject of this bibliography are here included.

Overstone had a great advantage in securing the assistance of McCulloch as Editor. McCulloch, whose knowledge of the literature of Political Economy was encyclopædic, rendered good service in making the selection both representative and complete.

These books, typographically, are models, and, in both matter and form, will remain things of bibliographical joy for ever.

In the preface to this volume McCulloch points out the distinction, so often lost sight of by writers on finance, between paper money and paper currency, the former being inconvertible and its value proportionate to the extent of its issue, progressively increasing on its curtailment or decreasing on its augmentation. The paper currency is, or should be, easily convertible. The tracts had been selected as exhibiting the principles which determine its value, but the enquiries into the nature of the measures to be adopted to give a practical effect to these principles had been dealt with in the briefest manner.

A detailed account of the tracts will be found under their respective dates.

1857

The two "Notes," Nos. V. and VIII., by McCulloch, may be more conveniently noticed here. The first, No. V., is on the "Suspension of Cash Payments at the B. of E. in 1797."

After the South Sea Bubble excitement had quieted down, "with the exception of a run for gold occasioned by "the advance of the Highlanders to Derby in 1745, there "was no considerable run on the Bank till 1792," in the Autumn of which year there was an acute crisis owing to a previous over-issue by the country Banks, many of which succumbed. When the disappearance of their issue had ensured the requisite contraction, the financial equilibrium was re-established, and a fairly healthy state of things prevailed till 1797, when, owing to fears of invasion, and consequent panic and hoarding, a run on the Bank set in, which resulted in the Suspension of Cash payments. During the reign of Paper Money, which lasted over twenty years, an enormous number of tracts were literally showered upon the public, especially at times when the Note went much below par. Of these pamphlets, luckily for the bibliographer, many have disappeared altogether. The writer has come across some which could have been written only by men absolutely ignorant of their subject: even with respect to the plainest facts, the views expressed are obviously distorted by self-interest, when not rendered incomprehensible by the imbecility of the writers. The question of depreciation was, however, so thoroughly threshed out in the Bullion Report of 1810, and, in the best of the contemporary publications on the subject, that every conceivable weak point of Paper Money may be said to have been detected and exposed.

The Recoinage difficulty of 1696, the Restriction period, the several Panics, and our own fifty years' experience of the Bank Act of 1844, furnish financial philosophers with an inexhaustible field of observation and research, in which any theory, however apparently novel, may be tested against known and indisputable facts. The present day Economist has, in addition to theoretical works, the benefit of the public speeches of practical men, the demands on whose time have precluded them from writing on the subject. This independent running comment is of the greatest value, and is an advantage of which the earlier workers were almost totally devoid.

1857—1858

The second "Note," No. VIII., is on the "State of the Exchange between London and Dublin from 1797 to 1804."

In 1689, the nominal value of the Irish shilling having been raised from 12d. to 13d., £108 : 6s. 8d. Irish money became equal to £100 only of British money; and the Exchange between Great Britain and Ireland was said to be at par when it was nominally 8⅓ per cent. against the latter. In some parts of Ulster, owing to a feeling against the Government, Bank Notes were very generally not accepted in payment of wages, or for goods; the landlords, too, stipulated for payment of rent in specie. Under these conditions the North of Ireland possessed a gold currency long after its disappearance in the South. This gave rise to curious anomalies; for instance, in December, 1803, when the exchange in Dublin on London was about 16 per cent., that of Belfast on London was about 5 per cent.; or, in other words, at the very time that the exchange between Dublin, which had a paper currency, and London was near 8 per cent. against Ireland, the Exchange between Belfast, which had a gold currency, and London was 3 per cent. in favour of Ireland. (At this time there was practically no gold in London in circulation.) Again, the rate between Dublin and Belfast was 10 per cent. in favour of the latter.

THE CURRENCY UNDER THE ACT OF 1844, together with observations on Joint Stock Banks and the causes and results of Commercial Convulsions.

(From the City Articles of the *Times*.) 1858.

The Articles are dated from 26th October, 1855, to 11th December, 1857.

Strongly against the suspension of the 1844 Act during pressure, however severe.

"Why should the currency be, even for a short time, "depreciated that unsound concerns should be propped?"

In the appendix, a speech of Lord Overstone (3rd December, 1857) is quoted. "If the Act had been main-"tained only twenty-four hours longer, the whole of the "vicious system would have been got rid of by the crumbling "to atoms of the institutions which fostered it."

Several excellent chapters on the contemporary discoveries of Gold.

1859—1860

On the Probable Fall in the Value of Gold.
    By Michel Chevalier.
    Translated from the French, with preface by R. Cobden.   Third Edition.   1859.

Advocates the retention of the Silver Standard in France. Has many suggestive references to the English Currency system.

The Writings of William Paterson, of Dumfriesshire, and a citizen of London; founder of the B. of E., and of the Darien Colony.
    Edited by Saxe Bannister.
    With Biographical Notices and facsimiles of Handwriting and Portrait.
    Second Edition.   Three vols.   1859.

This book contains a large amount of raw material towards the construction of a complete biography, but it remains, unfortunately, a chaotic mass of facts, the result of careful and conscientious investigation, with no organic unity.

In fact, in writing the short notice of Paterson's life appended to this volume, it has frequently been found easier to go to original sources than to wade through Bannister's book which he himself terms a *moles indigesta*.

Memoirs of a Banking House.
        By the late Sir Wm. Forbes, Bt., of Pitsligo.
                                                    1860.

A graphically written history of the House of Coutts & Co., of Edinburgh, the parent house of the banks of Coutts & Co., and Herries & Co., of London.

Forbes, who was born 1739, and died in 1806, finished the manuscript in 1803. It did not, however, get into print till published by Robert Chambers, in 1860, with an introductory notice by himself. Tells how Circular Notes

1860—1863

were invented by Sir Robert Herries in 1772. A capital account of the effects of the panic of 1797 in Scotland.

This fascinating book is a most valuable contribution to the History of Finance—a sort of Evelyn's Diary of Banking.

THE BANK ACT OF 1844, and free trade in Gold not incompatible with our standard of value, and the true remedy for ruinous fluctuations in prices, and in the Bank rate of discount.

By Henry Brookes (late editor, Bankers' Circular). 1861.

REASONS FOR AN ALTERATION IN THE LEGAL TENDER, AND A REFORM IN THE CURRENCY.

By Robert Slater. Fifth Edition. 1861.

THE BANK ACT, AND THE CURRENCY CORRESPONDENCE BETWEEN RT. HON. LORD OVERSTONE AND HENRY BROOKES, ESQ. 1862.

His Lordship sticks to the point, and holds his own.

This and the two preceding tracts were republished in one volume in 1862.

THE MYSTERY OF MONEY EXPLAINED AND ILLUSTRATED BY THE MONETARY HISTORY OF ENGLAND, from the Norman Conquest to the present time.

Second Edition. 1863.

Advocates bimetallism and the removal of the Bank from State control as better for all, it being unlikely, for its own sake, that the Bank would do anything tending to depreciate the value of its Notes.

In spite of its fanciful title and occasional oddity there is some good work in this book.

1863—1865

A Dictionary of Political Economy.—Biographical, Bibliographical, Historical and Practical.

H. Dunning Macleod.   1863.

Of this work, encyclopædic in design, only the first volume seems to have been published — A to Cu. It contains important articles on Banking in England and many other countries, and bibliographical lists on the subject.

La Question des Banques.   L. Wolowski, Paris.
1864.

The Birthplace and Parentage of William Paterson, founder of the B. of E., and projector of the Darien Scheme.

Wm. Pagan (Edinburgh).   1865.

The Author discovered in an "old Scotch land register" incontrovertible evidence that William Paterson was the son of John Paterson, in Skipmyre, parish of Trailflatt, now Tinwald, Dumfriesshire. He enlarges upon this.

Stories of Banks and Bankers.
Frederick Martin.   1865.

This little book is really a popular and anecdotal history of Banking in England, from the time of the goldsmiths' "running cashes" up to 1865, when the deposits in the nine principal Joint Stock Banks in London stood at £67,377,556.

A slight sketch is given of the Bank in its early "Paterson" days. Sir Henry Furnese, one of the first Directors of the concern, seems to have been a sort of seventeenth century Rothschild. He maintained, at his private expense, a complete and perfect train of intelligence through Holland, France, Flanders and Germany. He was in many instances ahead of the Government mail, as in the news of the fall of Namur, and had the full advantage of the market which his energy deserved.

1865—1867

Sir Robert Clayton, who was on the Board in 1702, was another celebrity, and was noted for the magnificence of his banquets, held in his palatial mansion in the Surrey hills, the rooms of which were wainscotted in cedar.

A Practical Treatise on Banking, Currency, and the Exchanges.

By Arthur Crump (formerly a clerk in the B. of E.) 1866.

The best section of this *multum in parvo* is that devoted to Bank Notes.

The B. of E. and the Organization of Credit in England.

Third Edition. 1867.

The most useful part of the book is the Appendix containing the Evidence of M. M. Isaac and Emile Pereire before the French Commission of enquiry into the management of the Bank of France; also an abstract of the American Free Banking Act, and an outline of a Joint Stock Bank on the New Principles.

La Banque d'Angleterre et les Banques d'Ecosse, par L. Wolowski, Paris. 1867.

Begins with an able criticism of the Restriction period (1797—1819).

" Il fallait se rendre compte des conditions et des " resultats, ... ainsi que les dangers qu'il faisait courir. " Le Bullion Report s'est acquitté de cette tâche avec une " hauteur de vues égale à la parfaite connaissance des données " pratiques." The panic of 1866, commencing with a graphic account of 11th May (Black Friday), is minutely described and commented on. The rest of the book is devoted to the consideration of the Scotch Bank Note Issue.

1868—1869

THE QUESTION OF SEIGNIORAGE AND CHARGE FOR COINING, AND THE REPORT OF THE ROYAL COMMISSION ON INTERNATIONAL COINAGE.

E. Seyd. 1868.

Contends that the Mint should be approached by the public without the Bank's intervention.

THE SCIENCE OF FINANCE. R. H. Patterson.

1868.

Advocates free trade in Banking, and total repeal of the Act of 1844 as better for the B. of E. and everybody else.

The B. of E., or any other Bank, to issue Notes to the extent they wish on their depositing Government Securities to the same amount with a State office. The author proposes to obviate the possible effects of a displacement of a certain amount of metallic currency thus caused by Banks keeping in their Banking departments large amounts of Foreign Securities, especially of those countries towards which an outflow of Gold might at any time be expected. In the case of internal panics, co-operation of the Banks themselves is advised, by lending each other part of their Issue, &c.

The suggestions for a Bank of Europe under the form of a sort of international clearing-house, and the manner of carrying it on, are as ingenious as they are interesting, but can hardly, at present, be held to be practicable, or within the scope of sound finance. Chapters on the 1866 panic and the National Debt. The B. of E., when it has been wise to do so, has assisted other Banks, and, in 1891, was well supported.

LA QUESTION MONETAIRE. Wolowski. 1869.

A Bimetallist.

Contains many letters and quotations from different authorities in support of his theory.

1870—1874

SPEECHES. LETTERS. ARTICLES, &c. ON THE GOLD COINAGE CONTROVERSY OF 1869.

Printed at the B. of E., December, 1870.

(For private circulation only.)

A short preface by Mr. R. W. Crawford, then Governor of the Bank.

An interesting and impartial selection from the *Times*, *Economist*, &c., of letters of Messrs. Thomson Hankey, J. G. Hubbard, T. Newman Hunt, E. Seyd, Sir John Lubbock and Professors Levi and Jevons, and several Extracts from Parliamentary Reports, &c.

An excellent idea of the points of the Controversy may be gathered from this work.

PRINCIPLES OF MONETARY LEGISLATION. with definite proposals for placing the sound and successful principles into permanent operation.

Richard Webster.   1874.

Proposes: 1. The permanent repeal of the restriction on the Bank Issue. 2. The abolition of the division of the Bank returns into Issue and Banking, and the amalgamation of the Cash reserve. 3. The abandonment of the restrictive system of regulating the Currency by the Foreign Exchanges. 4. That the State should place one or two permanent Directors on the Bank Board, &c., &c.

THE B. of E. NOTE ISSUE AND ITS ERROR. An Address to the holders of Bank Stock, and to Bankers and Economists generally.

E. Seyd.   1874.

Urges that B. of E. dividends have not increased as those of other Banks have. Argues that the Bank's position would be improved by making the amount of the fiduciary issue capable of increase, or decrease, in accordance with temporary conditions, and by the reduction of the present large reserve to a temporary small "indicating" reserve.

1875—1876

MONEY, AND THE MECHANISM OF EXCHANGE.
W. S. Jevons. 1875.

This volume, which is one of the International Scientific Series, gives a general account of the subject, by no means forgetting the B. of E.

A HANDBOOK OF LONDON BANKERS, with some account of their predecessors, the early Goldsmiths, together with Lists of Bankers from the earliest one printed in 1677, to that of the London Post Office Directory of 1876.
F. G. Hilton Price, F.S.A., (a partner in Messrs. Childs' Bank). 1876.
Enlarged Edition. 1890-1.

The various headings are arranged alphabetically. The notices of the older houses give an amount of information otherwise inaccessible, the collection of which must have entailed much tedious labour.

CURRENCY AND BANKING. Bonamy Price. 1876.

With respect to the 1844 Act, he would place the office of Issue in Somerset House, or Whitehall, that the world might understand the State to be the real issuer.

OBSERVATIONS ON A TABLE, showing the Balance of Account between the Mercantile Public and the B. of E. from 1844 to 1857.
William Langton. Salford. 1876.

OBSERVATIONS ON A CONTINUATION TABLE AND CHART, shewing the Balance of Account between the Mercantile Public and the B. of E., 1844–1875, with special reference to its course in the years 1866–1875.
Henry Baker. Salford. 1876.

This, and the preceding paper, which include several illustrative tables, diagrams and charts, were read before the Manchester Statistical Society, and the two, together with Jevons' "Frequent Autumnal Pressure, &c.," contained

1876—1879

in "Investigations in Currency, &c.," 1884 (*q.v.*), set forth with much clearness the periodicity of the high and low "pressure in the Money Market" as exhibited in the relations between the Public and the Bank.

Langton testifies to the Bank's public spirit during the 1857 crisis, and considers it "beyond all praise."

THE ELEMENTS OF BANKING.
H. D. Macleod. Fourth Edition. 1878.

Thirty-four pages are devoted to a consideration of the 1844 Act. The summing-up is that "the true criterion of "the proper quantity of paper currency was not its numerical "amount, but the state of the Foreign Exchanges and the "market price of Gold and Bullion."

Raising the rate of Discount is insisted on as "the true "supreme power of controlling the Exchanges and the "paper currency."

BANKING REFORM. AN ESSAY ON PROMINENT BANKING DANGERS AND THE REMEDIES THEY DEMAND.
A. J. Wilson. 1879.

Advocates that Banks of Issue should deposit Securities with the Government sufficient to cover their circulation, the holder of a Bank Note being, in a peculiar manner, entitled to protection.

INTERNATIONAL MONETARY CONFERENCE held in compliance with the invitation extended to certain Governments of Europe by the Government of the United States, in pursuance of the second section of the Act of Congress, 26th February, 1878.
Washington. Government Printing Office. 1879.

This relates to the International Monetary Conference (in Paris) of 1878, and gives an account of the proceedings and exhibits, followed by the Report of the American Commission, and an appendix containing correspondence

1879—1881

submitted to the Department of State by Mr. Fenton, and historical material, for the study of Monetary Policy, collected by S. Dana Horton.

It further contains a list of "Official publications concerning money" of different European Nations and the United States of America, and of modern treatises on Money, in various languages. This catalogue extends over twenty closely-printed 8vo. pages, and includes the names of the principal works published between 1791 and 1879, together with "The proceedings of the International Money Conference "of 1867." A copious general index to its 920 pages completes the work.

A most useful book to the student of the Bimetallic question, not only on account of the Report but of the valuable historical and other material illustrating it.

THE HISTORY, LAW AND PRACTICE OF BANKING IN IRELAND, with an introductory Historical Sketch, and an Appendix of Statutes.

Charles M. Collins, Barrister-at-Law. Dublin. 1881.

A large amount of condensed information with respect to the History of Banking in general, and especially in Ireland, and a short chapter (8 pages) on the B. of E.

The following illustrations of Irish humour are worth noting:—

In 1798, the Dublin mob, who had conceived a hatred of the head of the firm of J. C. Beresford & Co., Bankers, with true Hibernian vengeance, collected and burned their Notes in order to ruin the house!

The form of a cheque drawn on the Bank of Latouche & Co. by Whaley, a then noted character in Ireland, known as "Buck" or "Jerusalem" Whaley, is unique:—

> "Dear Mr Latouche
> Pray open your pouch,
> And give my heart's darling *
> One thousand pounds sterling."

* His wife, probably. Mr. Collins suggests.

1881

PATRIOTS IN ARMS. Addresses and Sermons by celebrated preachers of the last century in praise of the Volunteer Movement, with an Introduction and interesting historical notes.

Thomas Preston, Ex-Lieutenant R.V.

1881.

The first Address in this unique book is "To the "Volunteer Association of the B. of E. upon the consecration "of its colours on 2nd September, 1799." By Rev. Richard Lloyd, A.M., Rector of Midhurst, in Sussex.

His final peroration is a remarkable example of rhetoric.

"You have long been the honourable and worthy guardians "of the wealth and credit of the Nation . . . . your "disinterested and independent conduct casts the greatest "lustre upon yourselves, whilst it affords security to the "country at large, and more especially to the B. of E., "the grand depository of the wealth not only of this but "also of other kingdoms.

"These colours, which I have had the honour to consecrate, "plead with a silent, but powerful, eloquence in behalf of "your King, your country, and all the various and inestimable "blessings to which I have alluded.

"They likewise serve as sacred emblems and elegant "memorials, through which you may contemplate the praise "and admiration with which your loyalty and zeal are "honoured by the fair sex,—the best and most amiable part "of the human race.

"The character of the lady who will present to you "these colours reflects additional splendour on their value, "and her presence on this public occasion, I am confident, "will add fresh ardour to your zeal and inspire you with "the most manly and generous sentiments. I conclude in "addressing you all, my honoured friends, in the sacred "and authoritative language of an Apostle, 'Watch ye, stand "'fast in the faith, quit you like men, be strong.'"

Even the *fin de siècle* young lions of the "*Gaily Bellograph*" can scarcely roar in this wise, and the Rev. R. Lloyd preached a hundred years ago!

1881

The following note by Lieutenant Preston is given on the B. of E. volunteers :—

 "This corps was formed by the Governors of the Bank,
"from amongst their own employés, in April, 1798; its
"special duty was to protect the premises and property of
"the Bank.

 "The members were not to receive pay for their military
"services, but the Governors of the Bank provided uniforms,
"accoutrements and arms.

 "Their strength was limited to 450, of all ranks, divided
"into eight companies of fifty privates each, two were
"called the wing companies and the remaining six were
"styled the battalion.

 "Their colours were presented to them (as above stated)
"2nd September, 1799, at Lord's Cricket Ground.

 "The interesting ceremony was performed by
"Mrs. Thornton, wife of Mr. Samuel Thornton, M.P.,
"Governor of the Bank.

 "The colours were beautifully ornamented with the
"figure of Britannia encircled with branches of palm and
"oak, and, on an embroidered label underneath, the motto
"'God save the King.'

 "On presenting the Colours to Lieut.-Col. John
"Whitmore, M.P. (a Director of the Bank), Mrs. Thornton
"spoke as follows :—

 "'Gentlemen, I cannot contemplate the present scene
"'without partaking in those gratifying emotions which
"'I am persuaded the spectacle must excite in the minds
"'of all who surround me. Where, but in the happy
"'land to which we belong, could such a spectacle be
"'exhibited?

 "'A land in which we behold men of all ranks, situations,
"'habits and professions, instead of declining and shrinking
"'back from labour and danger, pressing forward, at whatever
"'expense of toil or peril, in the defence of their King and
"'Country. Our enemies had vainly flattered themselves
"'that military exertions were foreign to the habits of
"'commercial men, but, in the estimation of our character,

1881

"'they had forgotten we were Britons. We have proved to them that under the ennobling influence of that unrivalled constitution, which, through the blessing of Providence, we enjoy, every rank and profession, together with its own peculiar habits, combines those qualities which, as Britons, are common to them all. You, gentlemen, have associated under the influence of these generous emotions. Let these Banners be the centre of your union and the memorial of your public zeal.

"'May the same spirit of energy and unanimity which has raised our country to its present eminence long continue, and may you, who have been so justly distinguished as the guardians of public credit, stand forth its zealous defenders, the protectors of commerce, and thereby the benefactors of mankind.'"

"Lieut.-Col. Whitmore made the following reply:—

"'Madam, The Bank Volunteers assembled here this day, though generally engaged in far different pursuits, felt, in common with their countrymen, that in the hour of danger they had other duties to fulfil; and in the enviable position of their commander, I have no hesitation to declare my firm reliance on them, fully persuaded that, consistent with the first great object of our association, the immediate protection of the Bank, they will shrink from no service which circumstances may require at their hands. The very elegant and impressive manner in which you, Madam, have reminded us of the important truth that we live under one of the freest and best constitutions in the world, gives a double value to the colours you have done us the honour to present to our regiment.

"'I feel an entire conviction that these colours will, in every extremity, be defended with not less spirit than we have engaged, and are well determined, to exert in defence of the large national treasures committed to our care, treasures not wrung from the oppressed, nor the spoils of plundered nations, but the voluntary tribute of the world to the industry, the enterprise, the honour and integrity of this happy country.'

1881—1882

"The names of the commissioned officers in the corps "at the time of the presentation of the colours were "Colonel Whitmore, Major and Adjutant James Reed; "Surgeon, Mr. Vaux. Grenadier Company: Capt. Mellish, "Lieutenants Bentley and Bradley.

"1st Battalion Co.: Capt. Puget,   Lieut. Best.
"2nd   ,,   ,, Lewis,   ,, Aslett.
"3rd   ,,   ,, Simeon,   ,, Browning.
"4th   ,,   ,, Champion,   ,, Shrubsole.
"5th   ,,   ,, M. Amyand,   ,, Corner.
"6th   ,,   ,, Langley,   ,, Collins.

"Light Infantry Company: Capt. Manning and Lieutenants "Newcomb and Daws.

"Ensigns: Triquet, Towle, Smart, Thomas, Hutchison and "Humble.

"The uniform is thus described: scarlet tunic; white "cross-belt; buff waistcoat and breeches; breastplate, oval "Britannia; cartouche box, Britannia in centre, with 'Bank "'Volunteers' around. Whole gaiters, Grenadiers & Battalion. "Short gaiters, Light Infantry Company.

"The Grenadiers wore fur caps, and the Battalion round "hats, with bearskin across and red-and-white feather. The "military committee consisted of the Colonel, Major, and "seven Captains, and was permanent during life."

THE HISTORY, PRINCIPLES AND PRACTICE OF BANKING.   J. W. Gilbart, F.R.S.

New Edition, revised to date by A. S. Michie.
1882.

This capital combination of the same Author's "History "of Banking," first published in 1827, and his "Practice of "Banking," is full of practical information, and is written in a lucid and elegant style.

A chronological sketch of the B. of E., and several chapters on her various functions. Gilbart was born 1794, became manager of the London and Westminster Bank on its foundation in 1834, and retired from service in 1860. His industrious and useful life came to a close in 1863.

1882—1884

Hints for Investors, being an explanation of the mode of transacting business on the Stock Exchange, with comments on the fluctuations and quarterly average prices of Consols since 1759, &c.

By W. M. Playford. (Sworn Broker.)

1882.

Gives a clear account of B. of E. practice at that time in respect to Transfers, Powers of Attorney, &c.

Our Clearing System and Clearing Houses.

W. Howarth, F. R. Hist. Soc.   1884.

Gives much information in a small space on a little-known, but exceedingly important, subject.

The early origin of the clearing system is lost in the obscurity of the past. The first ascertained fact is that Messrs. Martin have an entry in their books, under date 1773, "Quarterly charge for use of clearing-room, 19s. 6d." In 1827, the Clearing-house adjoined and formed part of the building in which Messrs. Smith, Payne & Co. carried on business. In 1841, the "House" removed to the present premises in Post Office Court.

Lawson dates the establishment of the clearing-house from 1755. An old guide-book, undated, but probably published early in this century, states that "the practice of clearing is said to be a century old," the Banks employing clerks called "Clearers," who used to settle their accounts on the top of a post in Lombard Street, or on each other's backs. They occasionally resorted to a Bank with a large recessed window, which was convenient to them, but not so to the Bank, as they were often summarily ejected on account of the noise they made.

There is a tradition that a convenient tavern was sometimes the scene of primitive clearing operations, which were probably instituted by the "clearers" themselves for their own convenience. The enormous advantages of the system were, however, so obvious, that, in 1810, separate premises for this special purpose were taken.

1884

Mr. Howarth has been unable to trace who the first Inspector was, but, in 1818, the post was filled by Mr. John White, from Vere & Co. (afterwards Fuller & Co., now merged in Parr's Bank, Limited), with a salary of £100 per annum. At first, transactions were settled in Notes and Gold, later on by Notes of £50 and of larger amounts, the difference under the last £50 being carried over to the next day.

The Private Banks kept the institution to themselves till 1854, when the increasing number and power of the Joint Stock Banks made it difficult to keep them out any longer. Just afterwards, another innovation was made by the settlement of accounts by drafts on the B. of E. In 1839, the average amount of Bank Notes used per diem for adjustment of Balances was £213,100; from this we can estimate at their real value the benefits of the present transfer system, which was originally suggested by Babbage, who was opposed by the majority of the Bankers. Derbyshire, who, for so many years was Inspector of the house, however, again took the matter forward, and, demonstrating the many advantages of the transfer system, was successful in procuring its adoption.

Now, a simple order for the amount owed by one Bank to another, after being passed by the Inspector, is handed to the B. of E., who transfer the sum to and from the accounts of the respective Banks. It is part of the system that all Clearing Banks should keep their chief reserves with the B. of E.

An account is given of the Paris, Berlin, New York, and our own provincial clearing-houses, together with practical suggestions for a local establishment for the Banks in the West End of London.

The amount cleared 15th February, 1882 (a Stock Exchange settling day), stood (1884) highest for any one day with £70,848,000, and all this without the use of a single coin or note.

The writer asks, "What amount would now" (1884) "be "necessary, supposing the old plan were still in force, when "our daily totals average £19,000,000?"

The following figures have been extracted from the Returns in the Journal of the Institute of Bankers to show

1884—1885

the difference between the present and the past of this great institution which, in such an eminent degree, has economised trouble, time and money, not only in the financial world itself, but in so many other departments of commerce.

000's omitted, thus: 1,000 = 1,000,000.

	Total Clearings.	Average, Ordinary day.	Consols Settling day.	Stock Exchange Settling day.
1839.	954,402	2,900	4,500	4,100
1868.	3,425,185	10,000	11,200	21,800
* 1888.	6,942,172	19,600	27,700	52,200
† 1890.	7,801,048	22,100	29,900	59,000
§ 1895.	7,592,886	21,800	28,800	54,400
1896.	7,571,853	22,100	31,700	48,500

* National Debt converted this year.
† Baring crisis in the late Autumn.
§ Speculation in South African enterprises.

INVESTIGATIONS IN CURRENCY AND FINANCE.
W. S. Jevons, F.R.S.   1884.
Edited, with an Introduction, by H. S. Foxwell.

This volume (published posthumously) includes much that touches the B. of E. It is fortunate that these essays have been collected and made available for general reference, instead of remaining buried in the journals of several different Societies. " The frequent Autumnal " pressure in the Money Market and the action of the " B. of E.," **1866**, and the paper on " Commercial Crises " and Sun Spots," **1878**, are both interesting. The diagrammatic Charts, showing the rise and fall of prices, are most useful, especially " A Diagram, showing the price of the " English Funds, the price of Wheat, the number of " Bankruptcies, and the rate of Discount, monthly, since 1731, " so far as the same have been ascertained." This was originally published in 1862, but has here been brought down to 1883. A list, covering 50 pages, of the titles of Works on Money, &c., from 1568 to 1882, is by no means the least valuable part of the work.

THE COUNTRY BANKER, his clients, cares and work, from an experience of 40 years.
George Rae.   1885.

An excellent little book. Has a good section on Reserves and Liability.

1886—1887

BIMETALLISM. An Address delivered by Mr. H. R. Grenfell (Ex-Governor of the B. of E.) in the Memorial Hall, Manchester, 16th Feb., 1886.

(Published at Manchester.)

Points out that Parliament and Press are given up to other matters, and that the Platform remains as the only available means of obtaining the attention the question deserves.

A general statement of the subject is then given.

THE PRINCIPLES OF BANKING, ITS UTILITY AND ECONOMY; with remarks on the Working and Management of the B. of E.

By Thomson Hankey, Esq., a Director (1835 to 1892) and formerly Governor of the B. of E.

Revised, as regards the working and management of the Bank, by the late Clifford Wigram, Esq., a Director (1862—1894, and at the time of his death, Deputy-Governor) of the Bank.

Fourth Edition. 1887.

This book, the first edition of which appeared in 1867, is an amplification of a Lecture delivered, in 1858, by Mr. Hankey to his constituents at Peterborough, for which city he was then Member.

It is especially interesting on account of its containing the only reliable published account of the practical working of the Bank, and is valuable from the authenticity of the information it affords, which is effectually guaranteed by the position of its authors.

The first section of the work deals with "Banking "in connection with the Currency and the B. of E." The second consists of "A Lecture delivered at Peterborough, " 29th November, 1858, on Banking, its Utility and Economy," and the third gives a " Descriptive account of the B. of E.," &c., &c.

1887

Mr. Hankey "feels more firmly convinced than ever "that the principles laid down for the regulation of the "Bank in 1844 are perfectly sound;" that they have been of great practical good, and that, if any change should be made, it will be in the "direction of placing the whole "issue of Bank Notes as a circulating medium (in part "substitution for gold coinage) on the same footing as that "of the B. of E." He gives a lucid account of the origin of the system embodied in the Act.

In 1840, the select Committee on Banks of Issue found that, in 1839 (a period of commercial distress), the amount of the circulation was £15,532,000. Deducting £800,000 for Post Bills, which this sum included, leaves it at £14,732,000. As the Banking and Issue were not then separated, £2,000,000 had to be added for use in the till of the future distinct Banking Department, making £16,732,000. This sum was assumed, under a departmental separation of functions, to be the minimum amount below which the action of the foreign exchanges could not reduce "the Notes out of the Issue Department."

£14,000,000 was taken as a safe limit to the amount of Notes which, under all conceivable circumstances, must remain in the hands of the public to fulfil their requirements as regards paper currency, and was, therefore, held to be issuable without a corresponding reserve of Bullion.

Mr. Hankey quotes from Torrens "On the operation of "the Bank Charter Act, 1847." (*q.v.*)

"The minimum amount which would be required to be "issued against bullion held in deposit would be £2,732,000; "and that as the reserve of bullion could not, under such "circumstances, be ever reduced below £2,732,000, the "convertibility of the circulation would be secured. The "correctness of these views has been fully borne out by "experience. Theory has been verified by fact. In so far "as regards the perfect convertibility of the circulation, "the anticipations of the framers of the Act have been "realized. From the period at which the Act came into "operation, up to the present time, the reserve of Bullion "in the Issue Department of the Bank has never been "reduced below £8,000,000."

1887

We may say, now (1897), that the basis of circulation is as firm as it has ever been. The amount of the "fiduciary issue" (*i.e.*, the part of the Note Issue based on Government Securities) has increased in amount to a small degree owing to the fact that the Bank is allowed, under the Act, to take up a proportion of the lapsed circulation of any country bank that has ceased to exist, or has given up its issue; the increase is thus accounted for. The authorised Country Bank Note Issue for England and Wales, in 1844, was £8,631,647; in June, 1892, it was £4,693,869 (the actual average on 4th June, 1892, £2,209,144), and on 7th November, 1896, the authorised stood at £3,491,895, the actual being £1,562,579.

All profit on additional fiduciary issue, after deducting expenses, goes to the public.

The third section is a "Descriptive account of the "various Departments of the Bank." This succinct account of the manifold duties of the presiding genius of the market shows, as far as is possible, how they are performed.

"The Issue Department requires no management "whatever.

"As every Bank Note issued beyond the sum of "£16,200,000 is represented by the Bullion in the vaults, "and the 16 millions itself is invested in Government "Securities, no risk can possibly occur with respect to this "department until the issue of Bank Notes is reduced to "that amount, which has never yet been the case."

In the, at present, inconceivable event of the circulation sinking below the limit of the "fiduciary issue," the liability could be met by selling the Government Securities in the Issue Department. The debt of £11,015,100, due from Government to the Bank, could then, with the approval of Parliament, by a mere book entry in the Stock Ledgers, be turned into Consols.

In case of sale, the payment for these Securities would be made in the Bank's own Notes, which could then be at once cancelled.

The following extract, and summarised notes, show the active part taken in the control of the establishment by the Governors and Directors :—

1887

"The Governor and Deputy-Governor are in daily attend-
"ance at the Bank, and there is also a daily Committee,
"consisting of three Directors, who meet at half-past
"eleven o'clock to receive reports of all proceedings at
"the Branches, see that the whole of the Securities of the
"preceding day have been lodged with the proper officers,
"take in or deliver gold or silver from the vaults, approve
"or reject Bills offered for discount, examine from time
"to time Securities deposited by customers, and attend
"generally to any work required by the Governors.

"The Chief Officers in the Bank are the Chief Accountant,
"taking cognizance of all Accounts, including the National
"Debt; the Chief Cashier, in charge of all matters relating
"to money payments or receipts; and the Secretary, whose
"duties are immediately connected with the Courts and
"Committees.

"As a building, the Bank covers nearly four acres of
"ground, and bears an estimated rental of £70,000 a year.

"Upwards of 1,160 persons are employed, including
"those at the Branches, porters, mechanics, machine
"boys, &c., and the salaries and wages amount to nearly
"£290,000 a year, besides pensions to superannuated clerks
"and others of £15,000 more."

The book contains tables showing the decline of the Reserve in the Autumn, and its increase in May and June; the curious monthly ebb and flow of Notes with the public, always larger at the beginning, and coming back to the Bank at the end of the month (the rate of discount makes no difference in this movement); the circulation of gold coin in the United Kingdom; and a List of Governors from 1694 to 1888.

The First Nine Years of the B. of E.

An enquiry into a weekly record of the price
of Bank Stock from 17th August, 1694, to
17th September, 1703.

J. E. Thorold Rogers. 1887.

The book is founded principally on J. Houghton's price lists, Luttrell's "Brief Relation" and contemporary tracts.

1887

The careful collation of these original sources in the hands of so competent an investigator has resulted in a most graphic and interesting volume.

Five useful Tables are appended :—

1. Weekly prices of Bank Stock, from 17th August, 1694, to 17th September, 1703.
2. Rates of the Exchange on Amsterdam.
3. Discount, or premium, of Bills of Exchange between London and Amsterdam.
4. Discount of Bank Bills.
5. Changes in the Value of Gold, Silver and Guineas.

The highest price of Bank Stock during the period, according to Houghton, was $148\frac{1}{4}$ on 15th March, 1700, and the lowest 51 in money, and $62\frac{1}{2}$ in Notes, on 5th February, 1697. The exact significance of these prices is perhaps a little uncertain as the Stock was not fully paid up until 24th July, 1697. The following are the dates of payment, viz :—

2nd July, 1694	25 per cent.
27th September, 1694	25 ,,
27th November, 1694	10 ,,
10th November 1696 but not completely paid until 24th July, 1697	20 ,,
24th July, 1697 (or shortly after), out of profits	20 ,,
	100 per cent.

It is clear that on the 5th February, 1697, the date of the lowest price, not more than 80 per cent. at the utmost had been paid, but, probably, the price was made on the basis of full payment as the quotations begin in August, 1694, with the price of 102.

Rogers attributes the low price to over-issue of paper by the Bank, which he considers excusable as the Government were then exercising great pressure on the corporation.

The Book has a good Index.

1891

THE THEORY OF CREDIT. Henry Dunning Macleod. 1891.

Vol. 2. part II. contains an exhaustive and interesting historical account of the B. of E. from the currency point of view; also sketches of the rise and progress of Banking in Scotland and in Ireland, and analyses of the commercial Crises since 1764.

He lays down the principles of a "complete" theory of credit, in which all facts should fall into their proper places, and, by the light of which, we may be enabled to deal effectually with any crisis that may occur in the future, in such a manner as to prevent it assuming disastrous proportions and, in the increasing complexity of the conditions of international modern commerce, becoming an overwhelming panic.

Whether there may not yet arise fresh factors in the creation of commercial crises, or whether the world has reached a sufficiently mature age to eliminate such further chances, it is, in our ignorance of the future, impossible to say; the treatment here, however, of the known realm of Economics is conscientiously thorough, and deserves the most careful consideration.

Mr. Macleod is fair to the Bank throughout. In his account of the Baring crisis of 1890, he becomes justifiably enthusiastic.

The subjoined extracts show his view of the position:—

" On the 8th November, the appalling intelligence was " made known to the Governor of the Bank that this great " house (Baring's) was in the extremest danger of stopping " payment, with liabilities to the amount of £21,000,000; " and that the most energetic measures must be taken " without a moment's delay to avert the catastrophe.

" The magnitude of the panic which would have ensued " if this house had been allowed to shut its doors may be " gauged by the fact that, in 1866, the liabilities of " Overend, Gurney & Co., which was up to that time the " most stupendous failure in the City, were only £10,000,000, " whereas those of Baring Bros. & Co. were £21,000,000.

1891

"Moreover, Overend, Gurney & Co.'s liabilities were
"entirely internal, whereas the paper of Baring Bros. & Co.
"was held by millions in foreign countries. It is not too
"much to say that if this house had been allowed to stop,
"it would have produced a monetary panic throughout the
"whole world.

"In this emergency, the Chancellor of the Exchequer
"was summoned in hot haste to give counsel in the City.
"Popular report attributes the measures taken chiefly to
"the wisdom of Mr. Lidderdale, the Governor. With
"magnificent energy, the Bank itself being utterly unable
"to meet the crisis unaided, the Joint Stock Banks in
"London, the Provinces, and in Scotland, were summoned
"to combine, and a guaranteed fund of £15,000,000 was
"subscribed for.

"Moreover, news of the danger would, not improbably,
"have brought on a panic and a run for Gold. Vast
"quantities of stock were thrown on the market, which
"reduced it lower than it had been for years, and far
"different from the halcyon days when Mr. Goschen
"effected his conversion. It is also said that some of the
"Joint Stock Banks contemplated ceasing to discount,
"which would have at once brought on a panic, and were
"only dissuaded from doing so by the peremptory and
"energetic remonstrances of the Governor.

"But, to provide against a possible panic, it was
"necessary to have a provision of Notes; and as, under
"the Bank Act of 1844, additional Notes could only be
"issued against an equal amount of gold, several millions
"of gold were required to be got together without a
"moment's delay.

"The Rate of Discount was six per cent., and the
"Bank did not dare to raise it higher, because, with its
"exceedingly restricted power of issue, raising the Rate
"of Discount would have been the very thing to aggravate
"the panic, and bring on the Bank a demand for Gold
"and Notes.

"Accordingly, the Bank contracted a loan for
"£3,000,000, for a short period, with the Bank of
"France, and £1,500,000 with St. Petersburg, and obtained

1891

" £500,000 from other quarters. It had, therefore, the
" power to issue £5,000,000 in Notes, and felt itself
" secure.

" By these energetic means, in such splendid contrast
" to the proceedings of the Bank on former occasions,
" it was at length announced that all the liabilities of
" Baring Bros. & Co. were protected, but at the cost
" of the liquidation of this world-renowned firm, and the
" frightful Monetary Panic was averted, which would have
" thrown all former ones into the shade.

" The nearest parallel to this crisis was that of 1838,
" when the greatest American houses were in danger, and
" the Bank promptly and instantly advanced £6,000,000,
" and averted a Monetary Panic."

Mr. Macleod makes, amongst others, the following
remarks:—

" That although, in ordinary times, the Rate of Discount
" is the true supreme power of controlling Credit and the
" Paper Currency, it is utterly too slow to attract millions
" of gold if required to be got together in a few days.

" That, while the Bank is bound to such a narrow
" restriction of its power of issuing Notes, raising the
" Rate of Discount too much will aggravate the panic and
" bring on a run for Notes and Gold.

" It gives the *coup de grâce* to the Restrictive theory,
" and shows that, when a great Commercial Crisis is
" imminent, the Banks must act together instantly and
" promptly, and energetically support the mercantile com-
" munity, and not wait till half the city is in ruins, as on
" former occasions.

" The Bank, on this occasion, was saved by the energetic
" measures of Mr. Lidderdale, who is entitled to the gratitude
" of the whole Banking and Mercantile community in the
" world, for his bold, prompt and energetic measures, which
" were the only ones possible under the circumstances."

An authentic account of the events that marked the
crisis of November, 1890, will be found in the "Journal of
" the Institute of Bankers" for January, 1891.

1891

A MONEY MARKET PRIMER AND KEY TO THE EXCHANGES, with Diagrams.

George Clare. 1891.

This book, although small, is one of the most clear and complete on the subject.

The chapters on the relations between the B. of E. and the Money Market, and those dealing with the effects of the Exchanges and International Bullion operations on the Reserve, are excellent.

It is a great advantage that the Author describes things as they are, and that he does not manipulate facts to establish a preconceived conclusion. Special pleading is a vice by no means rare amongst financial theorists.

CHAPTERS ON THE THEORY AND HISTORY OF BANKING.

C. F. Dunbar. 1891.

"A little and good" book, with chapters on B. of E., Banks of Amsterdam and France, and the Reichsbank of Germany. Is generally up to date.

A HISTORY OF THE CIVIL SERVICE RIFLE VOLUNTEERS (including the Volunteers of the B. of E.)

Edward Merrick, Lieut. C.S.R.V. 1891.

The B. of E. Corps was enrolled, originally, in 1798 and, in 1804, it numbered 433, with a "Supplementary Corps" of 122; their parades were held at 7 or 8 a.m.

"The most notable period in their history appears to "have been in 1812, at the time of the assassination of "Perceval in the House of Commons;" when it was considered necessary for them to be under arms to guard the Bank night and day.

A general disbandment of Volunteers (including the Bank Corps) took place, in 1814, at the peace.

1891

In 1859, the Volunteer movement recommenced, and the C. S. R. V. Corps was started.

"An important event occurred in the History of the
" Corps, in 1866, in the foundation of a new company
" composed of members of the clerical establishment of
" the B. of E.

" The Bank had, as yet, taken no active part in
" the Volunteer movement, but, the Directors, following
" the traditions of their predecessors of the last century,
" were very favourably inclined towards it. It was with
" little difficulty, therefore, that Mr. Kingsmill, to whose
" energy the foundation of the Corps was principally due,
" succeeded in recruiting a sufficiently large contingent to
" make them an acceptable acquisition to any leading
" Metropolitan Corps.

" An attempt was made to draw them into the ranks
" of the London Rifle Brigade. Although not servants of
" the Crown, however, it was felt that there were bonds
" of affinity which drew them closer to the Civil Service
" than to any other Corps. Lord Bury's (C.O.) sanction
" was readily obtained, and in July, 1866, they joined,
" 140 strong, under the command of one of the Directors
" of the Bank, Captain J. P. Currie, ... and took
" rank, after the Admiralty, as the "K" Company.

" In 1875, a new Corps (one of the last raised in
" Middlesex) was formed from the porters and subordinate
" establishment of the B. of E. After the disbandment of
" the Bank Volunteers, in 1814, the Directors still considered
" it advisable to train a certain number of their employés
" to the use of arms, to be employed, if necessary, for the
" use of the Bank. Their porters and messengers were
" specially selected with a view to this purpose, and arms
" and uniforms were provided by the Bank. The year 1875
" found them a rather antiquated body of men, armed with
" the 'Brown Bess' musket. At this period, efforts were
" successfully made to bring them within the scope of
" the Volunteer regulations, and they were enrolled as the
" 50th Middlesex—afterwards changed to the 25th.

1891—1894

"The Corps consisted of one Company only, about "100 strong, under the command of Captain Gray (late "Chief Accountant of the Bank)."

The uniform is dark green, with busby, of the Rifle Brigade; the Company is attached, for battalion drill purposes, to the Civil Service Corps.

THE THEORY OF THE FOREIGN EXCHANGES. Rt. Hon. G. J. Goschen, M.P. 16th Edition.
1894.

The earliest Edition which the compiler has been able to examine is the Third, published in 1864, which contains the preface to the Second, dated October, 1863, and an Introduction (presumably to the First Edition) dated 1861.

It would be superfluous to give a detailed account of this well-known work, which still remains the best book on the subject.

A HISTORY OF BANKS, BANKERS, AND BANKING, IN NORTHUMBERLAND, DURHAM, AND NORTH YORKSHIRE, illustrating the Commercial Development of the North of England, from 1755 to 1894, with numerous Portraits, Facsimiles of Notes, Signatures, Documents, &c.

By Maberly Phillips, Associate of the Institute of Bankers, Member of the Council of the Society of Antiquaries of Newcastle-upon-Tyne.

London: Effingham Wilson & Co., Royal Exchange.

Printed by Andrew Dickson, 30 & 32, High Bridge, Newcastle-upon-Tyne. 1894.

In this excellent book no possible source of information seems to have been neglected by the writer, who has been for many years a member of the staff of the Newcastle Branch, B. of E., of which he gives a most interesting

1894

account. The Branch was opened on 21st April, 1828, and the Newcastle Bankers offered the strongest opposition to its establishment.

The Town Chamber of Commerce, after a very full meeting, memorialised the Governor and Company, who answered that they saw "no reason to alter the intention " of establishing a Branch Bank in that town." The business at first was small, the stock of Notes was injured by the dampness of the premises, the agent was annoyed by the dead cats, &c. thrown over the wall, and the neighbours' children were such a nuisance that, "for a shilling a week, " an old woman was employed to drive them away from " the doorstep."

In 1838, the Branch was removed to the fine premises in Grey Street, the business having greatly improved and the staff having been increased, and, in 1841, the new house was enlarged.

The crises of 1847 and 1857 were severely felt in Newcastle, and caused great pressure of work at the Branch; during several months the day's work was frequently not closed before midnight.

In 1872, principally through the influence of Mr. D. H. Goddard, who was agent at that time, the Newcastle Bankers' Clearing-house was established.

A concise History of Provincial Banking in England occupies 132 pages, the rest of the work being devoted to a review of the North Country Banks, with portraits of the partners, sketches of the premises, and many tit-bits of local information.

NATIONAL DEBT.

NATIONAL DEBT.

1701

The Villainy of Stockjobbers Detected, and the causes of the late run upon the Bank, and Bankers, discovered and considered.

(Daniel Defoe)   1701.

The particular "villainy" which drew down upon the Stockjobbers the wrath of the versatile author of "Robinson Crusoe" was the "rigging" up and down of the Stocks of the two rival East India Companies, the "Old" and the "New," one against the other.

"The old East India Stock, by the arts of these "unaccountable people, has within ten years or thereabouts, "without any material difference in the nominal value, been "sold at from £300 per cent. to £37 per cent." He complains that one set of men in the old Company hoarded cash which was then very scarce, and another "set in the same lot" hoarded Bank Bills to the amount of the £300,000. They (the Stockjobbers) started a run on the Bank and spread wild rumours to gain their ends. There seems to be something familiar to us in this statement.

He hopes, however, that all this "hurricane may yet fall "on themselves, and it were only to be wished that the "fall of Stocks would affect none but such as have "encouraged this destructive Hydra, this new corporation "of Hell, Stockjobbery."

The tract is given in the list of his works in the "Life of Defoe," by C. Chalmers. Halkett and Lang in their Dictionary of Anonymous Works confirm the fact of Defoe's authorship of the tract, and mention Wilson's "Life of Defoe" as their authority.

1710—1717

AN ESSAY ON PUBLICK CREDIT, being an enquiry how the Publick Credit comes to depend upon the change of the Ministry, or the dissolutions of Parliaments; and whether it does so or no. With an Argument proving that the Publick Credit may be upheld and maintained in this nation, and perhaps brought to a greater height than it ever yet arrived at, though all the changes or dissolutions already made, pretended to, and now discoursed of, should come to pass in the world. 1710.

McCulloch, in the preface to the volume containing the reprint of this tract, says that it is supposed to be by Harley, Earl of Oxford, and that it was referred to by the first Marquis of Lansdowne in the debates on Pitt's Sinking Fund in 1786.

The following definition is as true as ever, and has certainly lost none of its significance: "Publick Credit " is the consequence of honourable, just, and punctual " management in the matter of funds and taxes, or loans " upon them. Where this goes before, credit always follows."

Re-printed in the Overstone Collection.

A LETTER TO A FRIEND, in which is shewn the inviolable nature of Publick Securities.
By a Lover of his Country. 1717.

The main cause which drew forth this protest is best stated in the Author's words: "Your project is to lower " their interests, or, which is the same thing, to tax these " Funds in order to raise money for, or lessen the debts of, " the Nation." The subject is well handled, especially considering the then comparative novelty of the funding system, *e.g.*, "Money (that is, Securities or Funds) ought " in common equity to bear a higher value, *i.e.*, to produce " a greater yearly increase, than land," as in the case of land the principal always remains, and "that the owner can " but lose his interest or rent for a year, besides the law " giving him priority over other creditors," &c.

This and the preceding tract, "An Essay on Publick " Credit," &c., serve as excellent introductions to the study of that subject, of which they take a good general view.

Re-printed in the Overstone Collection.

1717—1726

A Collection of Treatises relating to the National Debt and Funds. The first of them dated April the 11th, 1717, and the last October the 30th, 1719, and also a Collection of Treatises relating to the South Sea Stock, &c.

By Archibald Hutcheson, of the Middle Temple, London, Esquire, and M.P. for Hastings in Sussex.

The first part (National Debt) of the Collection contains eight main Treatises and several sub-divisions, very precisely written, giving the author's ideas on the subject, and his discussions thereon with a Mr. Crookshanks. Hutcheson was in favour of each one paying off his own proportion of the Debt forthwith.

Hume refers to the book in his "Essay on Public Credit," and exposes the weak points of the scheme. The title of the seventh Treatise, viz., "A short abstract of 7 of my 8 states to which Mr. Crookshanks has objected little," sufficiently exemplifies the minutely detailed character of the style.

An Essay on the Publick Debts of this Kingdom, wherein the importance of discharging them is considered, the provisions for that purpose by the Sinking Fund, and the progress therein hitherto made, are stated and explained; the sufficiency of those provisions are demonstrated, some general mistakes about the nature and efficacy of this expedient examined and removed, and the progress of the Sinking Fund described and computed from Midsummer, 1727. To which is subjoined an Enquiry into the general convenience of reducing further the interest on our Public Debts below £4 per cent. per annum. In a letter to a Member of the House of Commons. Third Edition. 1726.

(Attributed to Sir Nathaniel Gould, an eminent merchant and Director of the B. of E.)

The virtues of the compound interest on a Sinking Fund are insisted on to an absurd extent. "Suppositions about

1726—1727

"the increase of the Publick Debt might be carried to the utmost extravagance, and still appear to be provided for by the above-mentioned Sinking Fund of £1,000,000, increasing at the rate of £4 per cent. compound interest, which, if it were worth while, might be shewed to be sufficient in about 105 years to pay off a debt of £1,575,000,000, allowing for the increase of the present debt of £50,000,000 by an addition of £15,000,000 in every year in which that Sinking Fund should be so applied." At the present-day, the enthusiasm of the "eminent merchant" is less, and his mathematical knowledge greater than those displayed by the writer of the above quoted passage. Luckily, the Ministry did not at once begin to borrow recklessly on the strength of these statements, of which nothing more was heard, after a year or two, for some considerable time.

Sixty years later, however, the seed bore fruit, when Dr. Price, in his "Appeal," &c., revived the idea, and tempted Pitt with it. The latter, with an empty Exchequer, was delighted with the notion, and asked the Doctor for a definite plan, which was adopted. So faithfully was it believed in, that the Acts for raising Loans during the Napoleonic wars actually contained clauses to restrain the growth of that increasing source of national wealth, the Sinking Fund.

Re-printed in the Overstone Collection.

A STATE OF THE NATIONAL DEBT AS IT STOOD 24TH DECEMBER, 1716, with the payments made towards the discharge of it out of the Sinking Fund, &c., compared with the Debt at Michaelmas, 1725.   1727.

Ascribed to Pulteney, afterwards Earl of Bath, then leader of the Opposition in the House of Commons.

This is the other side of the question. It traverses the statements made in the preceding tract as to some of the Debt having been recently paid off, and accuses the author of tempting the Nation to new debts by showing such an easy way, in the Sinking Fund, of paying off old ones.

Re-printed in the Overstone Collection.

1727

A Defence of an "Essay on the Publick "Debts of this Kingdom, &c.," in answer to a pamphlet entitled "A State of the National "Debt, &c."

By the Author of the "Essay."   1727.

This is a rejoinder, reasserting the controverted statements, and explaining those found "incomprehensible" by his opponent. The acuteness of the situation is shown in the following extract from the "History and Proceedings "of the House of Commons," Vol. 5:—

February 23rd, 1727-28, the "Committee of Supply "resolved to raise £1,700,000 on the coal-duty. Hereupon "Mr. Pulteney observed that the shifting of funds was but "perpetuating taxes, and putting off the evil day, and that, "notwithstanding the great merit that some had built on "the sinking fund, it appeared that the National Debt had "been increased since the setting up of that pompous project. "On which Sir Nathaniel Gould, an eminent merchant, said "he apprehended that gentleman had his notions out of a "treatise entitled 'A State of the National Debt,' supposed "to be written by that very gentleman, but that if he "(Sir N. Gould) understood anything, it was numbers, and "he durst pawn his credit to prove that author's calculations "and inferences to be false. To this Mr. Pulteney replied "that he took them to be right, and that he would likewise "pawn his credit to make good his assertion. Upon this, "Sir Robert Walpole took up the cudgels, and said he would "maintain what Sir N. Gould had advanced. Mr. Hungerford, "however, in a jocular speech, restored the House to its "good humour."

The matter attracted considerable public attention, both from the national interest in the question and the high standing of the disputants.

It appears that so excessively complicated was the system of State book-keeping at this time, that it was really extremely difficult to determine whether the Debt had increased or decreased. This curious state of affairs eventually led to Sir Robert Walpole laying the following report before the House.

Re-printed in the Overstone Collection.

1728—1735

REPRESENTATION OF THE HOUSE OF COMMONS TO H. M. GEORGE II., SHOWING THE STATE OF THE NATIONAL DEBTS IN 1716 AND 1726.

Commons Journal, 8th April, **1728.**

It appears from this that there had really been a decrease in the Debt of £2,698,416 9s. 7¾d., and "that this Sinking "Fund is risen to, and may be reasonably estimated at "£1,200,000 or thereabouts."

After referring to the awkward state of affairs abroad and sundry disturbances at home, he winds up with, "If, "notwithstanding these and many other difficulties which "we laboured under, and while the Sinking Fund was yet "in its infancy, and so much less than it now is, we have "been able to diminish the National Debts so much already, "what may we not hope for in regard to a more speedy "and sensible discharge of them for the future, now the "Sinking Fund is greatly increased," &c., &c.

It is difficult to know whether this was a mere ministerial flourish or whether Walpole really regarded the Debt as within, at any rate, a calculable period of extinction.

The Sinking Fund was soon, however, tampered with. In 1733 it was charged with £500,000, in 1734 with £1,200,000, and was again further heavily mortgaged, in 1736, in spite of a strong protest by the Peers in 1733.

Re-printed in the Overstone Collection.

AN ENQUIRY INTO THE CONDUCT OF OUR DOMESTIC AFFAIRS from 1721 to Christmas, 1733, in which the case of our National Debts, the Sinking Fund, &c., are particularly considered. **1734.**

SOME CONSIDERATIONS CONCERNING THE PUBLIC FUNDS, THE PUBLIC REVENUES AND THE ANNUAL SUPPLIES, occasioned by a late pamphlet, entitled, "An Enquiry, &c." **1735.**

1735—1750

THE CASE OF THE SINKING FUND AND THE RIGHT OF THE PUBLIC CREDITORS TO IT CONSIDERED, &c., being a Defence of "An Enquiry, &c.," and a full reply to a late pamphlet entitled "Some Considerations, &c."
1735.

AN ESSAY ON THE SINKING FUND, wherein the nature thereof is fully explained, and the Right of the Public to that Fund asserted and maintained. 1736.

A SURVEY OF THE NATIONAL DEBTS, THE SINKING FUND, THE CIVIL LIST, &c.
Inscribed to Sir John Phillipps, Bart. 1745.

CONSIDERATIONS ON THE PROPOSAL FOR REDUCING THE INTEREST ON THE NATIONAL DEBT.
By Sir John Barnard, M.P. 1750.

In favour of reduction.

AN ESSAY ON THE NATIONAL DEBT AND NATIONAL CAPITAL, or the Account truly stated, Debtor and Creditor, &c.
By Andrew Hooke, Esq., Bristol. 1750.

An interesting tract, protesting against the alarmist views prevailing at the time, respecting the amount of the National Debt. The work appears to have received no attention from the writer's contemporaries.

He attempts an estimate of the capital and income of England and Wales (Scotland?) in 1750, working from the figures of Petty and Davenant, and puts the capital at £1,000,000,000, and the income at £100,000,000. He points out that according to these computations, the National Debt was then a twelfth part of the capital of

1750—1751

the nation, and its interest a thirtieth part of the national income. The population he places at 10,000,000, "as 'tis generally computed," no doubt greatly in excess of the fact.

The writer goes on to propound a plan for liquidating the National Debt, by the creation of terminable annuities, a plan much in favour a very few years ago. The tract exhibits little original research, but shows some breadth of view and acumen.

THE HISTORY OF OUR NATIONAL DEBTS AND TAXES, from the year 1688 to the present time.
1751.

In four parts; the last published in 1753; about 400 pp. altogether. The author explains that "a large number of "authentic accounts relating to the Public Expense, Debts, "and Taxes of this nation, having lately, by accident, "fallen into his hands," induced him to make further investigation and publish his remarks, which he hopes will establish "a maxim observed by all wise nations, but "exploded by all wicked ministers." That the Annual Expense ought never to exceed the Annual Revenue. He computes that at the time of the Revolution the total income of the country from taxation amounted to very little over £2,000,000, and yet, with this revenue, King James supported his Civil List, kept a formidable Navy ready to put to sea, an Army of near 30,000 men "at land," and saved money yearly, if we can credit an account of the Issues of his Revenue, given in the same Session of Parliament, which amounted to no more at a medium than £1,699,363 2s. 9d., therefore it is probable he had large sums of money lodged in private hands somewhere or other. He gives full particulars of the supplies granted for the service of each year, and then explains and discusses the grants and the policy of the country very fully.

The book was re-published in 1761, with the title "The History of our Customs, Aids, Subsidies, National Debts and Taxes, from William the Conqueror to the present year, 1761."

The earlier edition is considered the better of the two.

1752—1756

OF PUBLIC CREDIT. By David Hume, Esq. 1752.
(From Essays, Moral, Political and Literary.)

He refers to the Ptolemies, Hezekiah, Plato, and other ancients as having had the foresight in good times to put away treasure against a possible evil coming time, and points out that now the process is reversed, and that we pawn the future to pay for the past, and prophesies the "eventual "violent death of our public credit."

He at first felt that this might occur in half a century, but, remembering that former prophets had been false, "he " contents himself with pointing out the event in general," without assigning any precise date, so as to be more cautious than "the astrologers in France, who were every year " foretelling the death of Henry IV. 'These fellows,' said " the king, 'must be right at last.'" It is remarkable that not even Hume foresaw the immense growth in national wealth which was so soon to take place, and that to an extent that rendered the interest on an enormously increased debt not only easily payable, but the burthen of the consequent taxation easily borne. It is curious that McCulloch reproduces verbatim portions of this essay in his "Taxation and Funding System" (1845) without the customary acknowledgment of inverted commas, though, in a footnote, he refers to Hume as his authority for certain of the statements.

Re-printed in the Overstone Collection.

ESSAYS ON THE PUBLIC DEBT, ON PAPER MONEY, AND ON FRUGALITY. Edinburgh. 1753.
By Patrick, fifth Lord Elibank.

Vide under date B. of E. section.

A SCHEME FOR PREVENTING A FURTHER INCREASE OF THE NATIONAL DEBT AND FOR REDUCING THE SAME, inscribed to the Earl of Chesterfield.
By Bourchier Cleeve. 1756.

1766—1772

A General View of England respecting Policy, &c., Debts, &c., from 1600—1762.
1766.

Remarks on Dr. Price's "Appeal to the "Public on the Subject of the National Debt," addressed to the Author. 1772.

Extracts from a Tract, entitled, "The "Challenge, or Patriotism put to the "Test."
In a letter to the Rev. Dr. Price.
Joseph Wimpey. 1772.

An able exposure of the fallacy of Price's Sinking Fund, (see Price, 1774). He points out that whilst the new Debt must increase as the old decreases it would simply be robbing Peter to pay Paul. It is strange that the writer's argument had no effect apparently on Price's opinions, nor in preventing the pernicious legislation that followed.

Re-printed in the Overstone Collection.

Note on the Sinking Fund Established by Mr. Pitt in 1786.
(See Overstone Tracts, 1857. XI.)

In this "Note" (no doubt by McCulloch, who edited the collection of reprints) the three schemes are given that Price submitted to Pitt when the latter, having succeeded in getting a surplus, consulted him. Pitt, influenced probably "by the very reasonable desire to avoid the imposition of "new taxes, adopted the third, and least efficient, of the "schemes suggested." It was carried into effect by Statute 26 Geo. III. cap. 31, which provides that £250,000 per quarter, or £1,000,000 per annum, shall be paid over to Commissioners, "who shall apply the same to the Reduction "of the National Debt, and to no other intent or purpose "whatsoever."

1773

Account of the National Debt, from Blackstone's Commentaries. Book I., cap. 8.

(Edition, 1773.)

This is enjoyable reading, compared with the usual controversial style of financial tracts, its comprehensiveness and lucidity are most refreshing. The passage disposing of the curious fallacy then current, and even in the present day not quite extinct, that the National Debt added to the national wealth by a sort of miraculous creation of credit warrants quotation.

"The quantity of property in the kingdom is greatly
" increased in idea, compared with former times, yet if we
" coolly consider it, not at all increased in reality.

"We may boast of large fortunes and quantities of money
" in the funds. But where does this money exist? It exists
" only in name, in paper, in public faith, in Parliamentary
" security; and that is undoubtedly sufficient for the creditors
" of the public to rely upon. But then, what is the pledge
" which public faith has pawned for the security of these
" debts? The land, the trade, and the personal industry
" of the subject; from which the money must arise that
" supplies the several taxes.

"In these, therefore, and these only, the property of the
" public creditors does really and intrinsically exist; and, of
" course, the land, the trade, and the personal industry of
" individuals are diminished in their true value just so much
" as they are pledged to answer. If A's income amounts to
" £100 per annum, and he is so far indebted to B that he pays
" him £50 per annum for his interest, one half of the value
" of A's property is transferred to B, the creditor. The
" creditor's property exists in the demand which he has
" upon the debtor, and nowhere else, and the debtor is only
" a trustee to his creditor for one half of the value of his
" income.

"In short, the property of a creditor of the public consists
" in a certain portion of the national taxes; by how much,
" therefore, he is the richer, by so much the nation which
" pays these taxes is the poorer."

1773—1774

He describes the Sinking Fund of his day, which consisted of "the surplusses of the three great national "funds, viz., the Aggregate, General, and South Sea Funds, "over and above the Interest and Annuities charged upon "them, and are directed by Statute 3 Geo. I. cap. 7, to "be carried together, and to attend the disposition of "Parliament."

The nett surplus of these three funds in 1768, with the addition of a few other smaller items, amounted to £2,009,000.

Re-printed in the Overstone Collection.

AN APPEAL TO THE PUBLIC ON THE SUBJECT OF THE NATIONAL DEBT. A New Edition, with an Appendix.

By Richard Price, D.D., F.R.S.

(First Edition, 1772.)   1774.

In this publication Dr. Price urged on the general attention what, in his opinion, was the only remedy for the ever-growing evil of the National Debt, viz., a Sinking Fund, and a non-alienable one, only, would suit the case. The author besides being a popular London preacher, had already earned no little reputation by some useful papers on actuarial subjects of considerable value to Insurance and Benefit Societies, and the plan placed before the public with ability by a known man, together with the general anxiety to learn of some scheme to avert the expected catastrophe of national bankruptcy, made the desire for a solution of the difficulty beget a belief that the plan contained it.

After expatiating on the enormous advantages to be gained by compound interest, he assumes the adequacy of a Sinking Fund formed on such a principle to redeem the Debt, and ingeniously shows that a partial alienation would pay it off better than a total.

"In most years it has been wholly alienated, and in "some years anticipated and mortgaged. Can we then "wonder it has done so little service?" He then makes this astounding statement. "From these observations the "truth of the following assertion will be very evident,

1774

"A State may without difficulty redeem all its debts by borrowing money for that purpose at an equal or even any higher rate of interest than the debts bear, and without providing any other Funds than such small ones as shall from year to year become necessary to pay the interest of the sums borrowed." He next shows how it is to be done, and inveighs against the Parliament, who had allowed the Sinking Fund to be diverted from its true function; he also states what was generally but erroneously believed, that the population was decreasing, and this he ascribes to the Debt. Price, like many public deceivers, had implicit belief in himself and his plan. "War while such a scheme was going on would increase its efficiency. . . . . Suppose, for instance, two wars should happen, one to begin five years hence, and to last ten years, and the other to begin thirty-five years hence, and to last also ten years, and both raising the interest of money in the Funds to £4 10s. per cent. It may be easily calculated that on these suppositions 145 millions instead of 99 millions would be paid off by such a scheme. But should it be suspended during the two wars, it would, in the same time, pay off no more than 40 millions."

He either did not or would not let himself see that wars do not pay their own expenses, and that an enormous new Debt would be growing all the while at £4 10s. per cent.

Pitt, pressed on one side by a nervous public, and attracted on the other by the specious reasonings of Price, accepted his suggestions, and carried the Sinking Fund scheme through Parliament.

Luckily for them both, owing to a surplus in the Revenue, for the first year or two of its life the Sinking Fund seemed to have done some good, a reduction of over ten millions being effected. This was, of course, put down to the credit of the scheme.

Re-printed in the Overstone Collection.

ANALYSIS OF THE SEVERAL BANK ANNUITIES.
Thomas Ashman.   1774.

1779—1784

CONSIDERATIONS ON THE PRESENT STATE OF PUBLIC AFFAIRS AND THE MEANS OF RAISING THE NECESSARY SUPPLIES.

 William Pulteney.   1779.

PROPOSALS FOR PAYING GREAT PART OF THE NATIONAL DEBT AND REDUCING TAXES IMMEDIATELY.

 Robert Bird.   1780.

ON THE DEBT OF THE NATION, compared with its Revenue and the impossibility of carrying on the War without Public Œconomy. 1781.

TRACTS BY JOHN, EARL OF STAIR, ON THE PUBLIC DEBTS OF THE KINGDOM. 1782.
 Pessimistic.

THE STATE OF THE PUBLIC DEBTS AND FINANCES AT SIGNING THE PRELIMINARY ARTICLES OF PEACE IN JANUARY, 1783.

 Richard Price, D.D., F.R.S.   1783.

POSTSCRIPT TO A PAMPHLET BY DR. PRICE ON THE STATE OF THE PUBLIC DEBTS AND FINANCES, &c., &c.   1784.

PLAN FOR REDUCING THE EXPENSES OF THE NATION AND GRADUALLY PAYING OFF THE NATIONAL DEBT.

 G Box.   1784.

1786—1787

THE NATIONAL DEBT PRODUCTIVE OF NATIONAL PROSPERITY. 1786.

The Author is apparently unable to distinguish between increase of the means of subsistence and the circulation of money; he imagines that the latter must necessarily increase prosperity, and that the National Debt acted as a circulating engine. Thus he proves his thesis to his own satisfaction.

A SHORT ADDRESS TO THE PUBLIC, containing some thoughts how the National Debt may be reduced, and all Home Taxes, including Land Tax, abolished.
William, Lord Newhaven. 1786.

Seems to suggest the imposition of a sort of Income Tax, which might, in time, yield a surplus large enough to effect the purpose in view.

CONSIDERATIONS ON THE ANNUAL MILLION BILL AND ON THE REAL AND IMAGINARY PROPERTIES OF A SINKING FUND. 1787.

A closely argued, well-written tract, but the public had no ears to hear with, and as in the case of Wimpey, fifteen years before, they would not listen. Price's promise of wealth was sweeter than prophetic warnings of poverty. "To return to the Surplus Bill. Parliament has engaged to "apply a million annually to redemption of Debts. If there "is no surplus, either the plan must drop to the ground, or "the million must be raised by new taxes or a new loan." Again. "Should new loans increase faster than taxes can "be provided to satisfy the Interests, no Sinking Fund "could be of service, but the Debt must increase as long as "any one could be found to trust.

"To reduce our debts . . . . a clear surplus must be "provided. Such a surplus can only be created in two "ways. . . . by taxes or by savings. . . . both almost "equally necessary, as the produce of either singly can have "but little effect."

Re-printed in the Overstone Collection.

1792—1795

A REVIEW OF DR. PRICE'S WRITINGS ON THE SUBJECT OF THE FINANCES OF THIS KINGDOM, to which are added the three plans communicated by him to Mr. Pitt in 1786, for Redeeming the National Debt.

    By William Morgan, Esq., F.R.S. (Actuary to the Equitable Insurance Company, and nephew to Dr. Price). **1792.**

A REVIEW OF DR. PRICE'S WRITINGS ON THE FINANCES OF GREAT BRITAIN, to which are added the three plans communicated to him by Mr. Pitt, in the year 1786, for Redeeming the National Debt: an account of the real state of the public income and expenditure from the establishment of the Consolidated Fund to the year 1791, and a Supplement carrying the account up to 1795, and stating the present amount of the Public Debt.

    (Second Edition.) Wm. Morgan, F.R.S. **1795.**

The author, as above stated, was Price's nephew, and Actuary to the Equitable Insurance Company. Without quotation of many of the calculations, &c., which our limits of space forbid, it is difficult to give an account of this book.

A LETTER TO THE RT. HON. WILLIAM PITT, CHANCELLOR OF THE EXCHEQUER, ON THE NATIONAL DEBT.

    Edward Tatham, D.D., Rector of Lincoln College, Oxford. **1795.**

Readable, but of little value; written in a rather inflated style, and teeming with patriotism, fine sentiment, and half truths. The writer considers the National Debt a public benefit, and ascribes the progress of the country during the eighteenth century to its influence in circulating capital—collecting it as taxes on the one hand, and paying it away

1795—1796

as interest on the other. He holds that the repayment of any large portion of the Debt "would unhinge property, order, and the State itself," and looks for a gradual decrease in its real burden through the tendency of money to depreciate in value.

As the shilling was formerly worth as much as twenty were at the time of his writing, so the constant accumulation of gold and silver must continue to reduce its value. The subscribers would have no cause of complaint. What they lent to the nation was money liable to a degradation in value. The quantity of money will naturally increase through the operation of commerce, and its value will decline in a corresponding degree.

The Sinking Fund would, he thinks, be much more profitably employed in the enclosure and cultivation of the Royal Forests, than in the redemption of debt. The author expresses a lofty contempt for the views of Adam Smith regarding National Debts.

"Instead of 'a ruinous system,' as the author of the 'Wealth of Nations' too often calls it, who loses large and comprehensive views in minute and narrow speculations, and whilst he is groping about after the shadow lets the body of truth escape out of his hands, the Funding System has been the great support and nourishment of the nation. Instead of 'gradually enfeebling the State,' according to his feeble comprehension, it has gradually strengthened and enriched it; and the general cause of the prosperity of Great Britain for ages past is to be found in the Funding System more than in any other resource, natural or artificial."

FACTS, &c., &c., RESPECTING THE NATIONAL DEBT. Second Edition. Wm. Morgan, F.R.S., &c.
1796.

AN ENQUIRY, &c., IN ANSWER TO MORGAN'S "FACTS, &c."
1796.

1796—1797

FACTS ADDRESSED TO THE SERIOUS ATTENTION OF THE PEOPLE OF GREAT BRITAIN RESPECTING THE EXPENSE OF THE WAR AND THE STATE OF THE NATIONAL DEBT.
    Second Edition. Wm. Morgan, F.R.S.
                                                  1796.

Remarks on Sinking Fund, &c.

AN ENQUIRY INTO THE STATE OF THE FINANCES OF GREAT BRITAIN IN ANSWER TO MR. MORGAN'S FACTS.
    N. Vansittart.   1796.

Says Morgan's facts were not facts; also that national resources had increased.

A LETTER TO THE RT. HON. WILLIAM PITT, CHANCELLOR OF THE EXCHEQUER, ON THE CONDUCT OF THE BANK DIRECTORS, with cursory Observations on Mr. Morgan's Pamphlets respecting the Expense of the War and the State of the National Debt.
    By a Proprietor of Bank Stock.   1796.

Complains that the Bank reduced its discounts unnecessarily and injured the Country Bankers in 1793. Looks on Morgan as pessimistic, and trusts that the "heart of every good "Englishman will suggest the answer that the true road to "peace is by a vigorous prosecution of the war."

AN APPEAL TO THE PEOPLE OF GREAT BRITAIN ON THE PRESENT ALARMING STATE OF THE PUBLIC FINANCES AND OF PUBLIC CREDIT.
    William Morgan, F.R.S.   1797.

1797—1802

A NEW SYSTEM OF FINANCE, PROVING THE DEFECTS OF THE PRESENT SYSTEM: that a saving may take place in the Public Income and Expenditure to the amount of near Ten Millions annually: Exposition of the consequences to the Public through their connection with the B. of E.: the baneful consequences of Stockjobbing: Astonishing hopes sustained by the Public that have enabled the Minister to carry on the Deception of Lessening the Public Debt: the unparalleled advantages given by the Minister to the Loan Mongers for Paper Credit in order to support the present ruinous War: £100 Securities in the £3 per Cents. given by the Minister, to receive £41 : 10s. 8d., to be sent to Germany for the support of the Emperor's Loan: together with a Reply to Messrs. Morgan and Vansittart on the subject of Finance: some remarks on Simon: the Stockbroker's letter to Mr. Alderman Curtis, late Lord Mayor of London: on the Iniquity of Private Tontines: Schemes for the Benefit of Age on the most reputable Establishments, a reasonable Compromise between Debtor and Creditor: a perfect Establishment for National Credit in future, and the People relieved from the most burthensome of their Taxes.

Thos. Fry (Author of the Guardian of Public Credit). 1797.

The title-page saves the trouble of any further indication of the character of the work.

A COMPARATIVE VIEW OF THE PUBLIC FINANCES FROM THE BEGINNING TO THE CLOSE OF THE LATE ADMINISTRATION.

Wm. Morgan, F.R.S. 1801.

ON THE PUBLIC FUNDS. Simeon Pope. 1802.

1802—1810

TERMS OF ALL THE LOANS THAT HAVE BEEN RAISED DURING THE LAST FIFTY YEARS.
J. J. Grellier.   1802.

A useful compendium.

SUBSTANCE OF LORD HENRY PETTY'S SPEECH IN THE HOUSE OF COMMONS PROPOSING HIS NEW PLAN OF FINANCE.   1807.

His Lordship afterwards became Marquis of Lansdowne. The scheme was only tried for one year, and then dropped.

Vide Hamilton's "Enquiry, &c." 1818.

AN ATTEMPT TO ASCERTAIN A THEORY FOR DETERMINING THE VALUE OF FUNDED PROPERTY.   1809.

There is more of interest in this pamphlet than the title would indicate.

THE HISTORY OF THE NATIONAL DEBT, from the Revolution in 1688 to the beginning of the year 1800. With a preliminary account of the debts contracted previous to that era.
By the late J. J. Grellier (Cashier to the Royal Exchange Assurance Co.)   1810.

The arrangement of this work is chronological; its author, who died before its completion, must have worked for many years to have accumulated the enormous mass of detailed information that the book contains. It gives the particulars with respect to any small loan with the same minuteness as the most important events relating to the whole Debt. This rather tends to render the book valuable only to the specialist. He usually speaks well of the Bank. *e.g.*, "an institution which, being under the direction " of men more intimately conversant in money transactions " than public ministers usually are, and more strongly " impressed with a sense of the necessity of maintaining an " inviolable punctuality in such transactions, has contributed " more than any other measure towards the establishment " and support of public credit."

1810—1818

The following extract concerns near neighbours of the B. of E.

"The Civil List was again in arrear, or, at least, was said to be so, for the House of Commons had no knowledge of such arrear previous to His Majesty's message of the 4th May, and the motion for an account of particulars was negatived. By the message His Majesty informed them of his intention to establish the two corporations of the Royal Exchange and London Assurance Companies, and hoped for their concurrence to confirm the privileges intended to be granted, and to enable him to apply the money which the Companies had agreed to advance to discharge the debts of his civil government; an Act for this purpose was accordingly passed, and the charters were executed 22nd June, 1720."

The Companies were to pay £300,000 each; half of this was, however, eventually remitted.

An Enquiry concerning the Rise, Progress, Redemption, Present State and Management of the National Debt of Great Britain and Ireland.

Robert Hamilton. Third Edition, enlarged.

(First Edition, 1813.) 1818.

This work, which was destined to destroy the confidence of the British public in its beloved Sinking Fund, was published (first edition) when the author had reached his seventieth year. He was born in Edinburgh in 1743, was Rector of the Academy of Perth 1769, and in 1779 was Professor of Mathematics in Aberdeen University. As he had in early life been in a banking house, he to some extent combined knowledge of theory with practice. He died in 1829, living just long enough to see his principles adopted by Sir H. Parnell's Finance Committee of 1828. The Act (10 Geo. IV. cap. 27), passed shortly afterwards, established a Sinking Fund in accordance with the Committee's recommendations.

1818

Hamilton begins by stating twelve first principles; it is only essential here to quote the last.

"The excess of revenue above expenditure is the only real Sinking Fund by which public debt can be discharged. The increase of the revenue, and the diminution of expense are the only means by which this Sinking Fund can be enlarged, and its operations rendered more effectual; and all schemes for discharging the national debt by sinking funds operating by compound interest, or in any other manner, unless so far as they are founded on this principle, are illusory."

He examines this and the preceding eleven, and exemplifies them in his clear and logical way, so as to be patent to the proverbial meanest capacity.

Part II. contains a History of the Public Debts of Great Britain, and an account of the various Sinking Funds, the first of which was Walpole's, established in 1716; this was worked more or less on the principle afterwards urged by Price, viz., that it was better always to devote the Fund to its original purpose; and if the money wanted for "Supply" fell short, then a fresh loan should be issued, or a new tax imposed, but the money for the Sinking Fund was still to be inviolate.

As might be expected, the temptation soon became too great for a ministry short of funds, and from 1733 it was so mortgaged and tampered with that its value was practically *nil*. Roughly speaking, in the seventy years from 1716 to 1786, there were twenty-five years of peace, during which only eight and a half millions were paid out of the Sinking Fund, any other discharge of the Debt being effected from other sources.

Pitt's Sinking Fund on Price's plan was formed in 1786, on the establishment of the Consolidated Fund, a million from which was handed each year to Commissioners for the Reduction of the National Debt.

In 1792 another Sinking Fund was established of one per cent. on the nominal capital of each Loan, to which the dividends on the capital redeemed by this fund were to be added. From 1798 to 1802 this plan was deviated from. In the latter year the two Sinking Funds were united, applicable to the discharge of the debts then existing.

1818

On all Loans subsequent to 1802 the system of a Sinking Fund of one per cent. was revived till 1813, with the exception of the Loan for 1807, when the Government adopted the system of Lord Henry Petty (Chancellor of the Exchequer, afterwards Marquis of Lansdowne) for that one year. But the Ministry was soon out, and the plan was finally dropped. It was a rather complicated system of mortgaging the war taxes, and Hamilton shows that the action of the compound interest was rather against the public in this scheme.

In 1813 Vansittart's plan of finance was brought forward. This was intended to relieve the public to some extent from the heavy burden of taxation to which they were subjected on account of the unrestrained action of the Sinking Fund, from which they had obtained as yet no benefit, and secure, if possible, the redemption of each Loan at a period not exceeding 45 years from its first issue.

The author examines each of these plans *seriatim*, and the clear light of his criticism shows up the weak points that the unaided eye of the public was unable to discern. It is difficult to find points which are not touched on by his principles, all the work being so thoroughly thought out. For example, " Whenever a nation does not tax to the
" amount of its expenditure, an increase of debt to a higher
" amount than the sum saved in taxes is inevitable, and in
" the comparison of different systems, those which impose the
" lightest taxes must always bring on an increase of debt
" to a still higher degree.

" In examining this (Vansittart's) and the other systems
" of finance, we have chiefly confined ourselves to a view of
" the effects expected from them during the first 16 years,
" or thereby, from their establishment. In the Tables
" annexed to the plan, their operation is traced for a much
" longer time. That of the Sinking Fund is extended as
" far as 1866, and we are informed that the remaining Debt
" will be redeemed according to the existing system in the
" year 1912, and according to the new system in the year
" 1875. . . . . It is morally impossible any system can be
" adhered to so long. Sir Robert Walpole's Sinking Fund
" was never supported with efficacy. Mr. Pitt's Sinking
" Fund commenced in 1786, and was corroborated in 1792,

1818

"considerably infringed on in 1798, underwent a great
"alteration in 1802, was laid aside for Lord H. Petty's plan
"in 1807, revived in 1808, and is now superseded by
"Mr. Vansittart's plan in 1813, and it may be almost
"certainly foreseen that measures different from those now
"proposed will be had recourse to by succeeding financiers.
"This will arise not only from the different views of different
"men, but from the change of circumstances which the
"fluctuation of human affairs always induces."

In the "General Observations on Sinking Funds" which follow, Hamilton calls attention to the fallacy of maintaining any sort of Sinking Fund whilst the expenditure exceeds the revenue, and a constant succession of fresh loans are being issued.

He also saw "That, although the National Debt has
"greatly increased, the means provided for its discharge
"have increased in a still higher degree, and therefore its
"present magnitude affords no cause of alarm."

He deals as well with the unfounded fears as to a heavy fall in prices from too rapid a decrease in taxation owing to the speedy repayment of the National Debt by the action of the Sinking Funds. Although, as he says, the Sinking Fund theorists claimed to have paid off £238,000,000 of Debt, or all the Debt contracted prior to 1786, in the beginning of 1813 a new debt had been contracted of £574,000,000.
"Does not this amount to the same as that we had paid
"no debt at all, but contracted an additional debt of
"£336,000,000?"

In his criticism on the system of funding by increase of capital, he calls up Price as a witness against himself, and quotes from the "Appeal":—"Were a person in private
"life to borrow £100 on condition that it should be reckoned
"£200 borrowed at £2 10s. per cent., he would, by subjecting
"himself to the necessity (if he ever discharged the debt) of
"paying double the sum received, gain somewhat of the air of
"borrowing at £2 10s. per cent., though he really borrowed
"at £5 per cent. But would such a person be thought in
"his senses?" (Price has said that the case of public borrowings was quite different.)

1818—1820

Now this actually represents what had been going on for years in the £3 per cents. During the period from 1793—1814 the sum raised was £157,650,000, the capital funded thereon being £267,804,500, the interest on which is £8,034,135, making the rate paid £5 2s. per cent. In the £3 per cent. Loan of 1804, £182 capital was granted for every £100 raised. "On an average of all the £3 per cent. Loans since the commencement of the war about £170 has been granted." He gives instances as well in the £4 and £5 per cents.

The last fifty pages of the work are taken up with notes explanatory of the statistics, and extracts from returns confirming the various statements. The book altogether is a fine piece of critical work, and the nation will always be indebted to the author for placing before it so clearly the important subject he deals with.

Re-printed in the Overstone Collection.

The B. of E. and the Sinking Fund, &c.
J. Grenfell. 1819.

Elements of a Plan for Liquidating the National Debts.
R. Heathfield. Sixth Edition. 1819.

Further Observations on Liquidating the National Debt, &c.
R. Heathfield. 1820.

A Plan for Reducing the Capital and the Annual Charge of the National Debt, &c., &c.
John Brickwood, Junior. 1820.

1822—1824

AN ADDRESS TO THE MEMBERS OF THE HOUSE OF COMMONS UPON, &c., and establishing an efficient Sinking Fund for the Redemption of the National Debt, with the outline of a plan for that purpose.

 By One of themselves. 1822.

REMARKS ON THE PRESENT STATE OF THE NATION, addressed to the Public, more particularly to the Members of both Houses of Parliament, pointing out an effectual mode of Liquidating the National Debt.

 By a man of Kent. 1822.

Interesting only as a sign of the times.

FAIRMAN ON THE FUNDS. Edited by B. Cohen. Second Edition. 8vo. London. 1824.

 The full title stands, "An Account of the Public Funds "transferable at the B. of E. and of the Stock of some "of the Principal Companies in London, with tables for "ascertaining the relative value of the different Government "Securities, and a History of the National Debt and "Sinking Fund."

 Has an excellently written chapter on the Advances made at various times by the Bank to the Government, and a statement giving amounts, dates, and Acts, and a summary of information on the Bank and Bank Stock from 1694 to date.

 Supplement to the above, bringing the account down to **1827**, "with a notice of the measures adopted during the late financial crisis (1826)," and accounts of the fluctuations in the Funds.

A FURTHER ENQUIRY INTO THE FORM OF OUR NATIONAL DEBT AND INTO THE MEANS AND PROSPECTS OF ITS REDEMPTION.

 François Corbaux. 1824.

1825—1830

AN ESSAY ON THE NATIONAL DEBT. John Rooke.
                                                1825.

FAIRMAN ON THE FUNDS. Supplement.   1827.
    (See 1824.)

ESSAY ON THE SUPPOSED ADVANTAGES OF A
    SINKING FUND.
        Third Edition.   1828.

By Lord Grenville, who herein recants his former creed as to the utility of a Sinking Fund, and gives in his adherence to the Hamilton School.

OBSERVATIONS ON LORD GRENVILLE'S ESSAY ON
    THE SINKING FUND.
        W. Boyd.   1828.

A LETTER TO LORD GRENVILLE ON THE SINKING
    FUND.
        T. P. Courtenay.   1828.

HISTORICAL VIEW OF THE SINKING FUND.
        P. Pusey.   1828.

A PLAIN STATEMENT OF SOME PARTICULARS OF
    THE FINANCIAL SITUATION OF THE UNITED
    KINGDOM, with brief remarks on the inutility
    of the Sinking Fund in the present state of the
    Revenue, with an Appendix.
        By C.   1828.
Practical.

A CALL TO THE WOMEN OF ALL RANKS IN
    THE BRITISH EMPIRE ON THE SUBJECT
    OF THE NATIONAL DEBT.   1830.

The author suggests that the Women of England should collect for a Voluntary Fund to pay off the National Debt !!!

1831—1845

The National Debt, its Evils and their Remedy.
By a Land and Fund Holder.   1831.

Interesting. Describes the financial history of the country during the previous 40 years in the somewhat familiar allegory of a rich young nobleman who comes into a fine estate and spends enormously beyond his means. Suggests that as the greater part of the Debt was subscribed in a depreciated currency, when, through the suspension of cash payments, the Bank Note was from 30 to 50 per cent. less valuable than gold, and as the welfare of the community at large is more important than the claims of the fund-holders, the interest paid to the latter should be reduced one-half, and that taxes should be remitted to a corresponding amount.

On the Public Debt, with a Plan for its Final Extinction.   1839.

Calls attention to the pressing necessity of at once taking measures to reduce the capital of the National Debt, and suggests its conversion into a series of Terminable Annuities, by which the whole Debt would be completely extinguished in one hundred years.

A Treatise on the Principles and Practical Influence of Taxation and the Funding System.
By J. R. McCulloch.   1845.

The only portion of the Treatise with which the Bibliography is concerned is the last, the Funding System. The subject is treated with such lucidity and breadth of knowledge that a brief synopsis may be permitted.

The problem of providing money for an emergency, and in this sense an emergency generally means war, has been variously solved by different peoples and different ages. The Ancient World was in favour of hoarding the surplus revenues of years of peace. It was left for modern science to discover the economic objections to this system; that it diminishes the working capital and means of employment of the nation, and modern politicians seem to favour, universally, an increase of taxation, accompanied or not by a loan.

1815

The different merits of these methods, increase of taxation and borrowing, have often been hotly discussed, but while either, or a combination of the two, may be right under certain circumstances, where the conditions are not in favour of any one, increase of taxation is to be preferred. This, however, postulates a strong Government, and a not over-burdened country.

The Borrowing or Funding System has given rise to several misconceptions. In its infancy the nature of the Public Debt was absurdly misunderstood. Bishop Berkeley spoke of it as a "mine of gold," but as Blackstone well points out, the National Debt does not increase the wealth of the country, but merely transfers it from one pocket to another, from the tax-payer to the Stockholder.

As a matter of fact the advantages of a public debt, the stimulus to invention and economy, the facilities for investing the smallest savings, the important businesses of banking and insurance, of which it is the condition, are outweighed by the disadvantage of the heavy taxes necessary to pay the interest, which reduce the rate of profit, cripple the public energies, and encourage the transfer of capital and skill to less heavily-taxed countries.

The adaptation of the Funding System to raising supplies, the readiness of capitalists to lend to the State, and the preference of the people to pay the interest instead of the principal in taxes are indisputable merits, but it is nugatory to suppose that the waste and profusion occasioned by a war can be counteracted except by the industry and economy of individuals. If A's share of the burden be £1,000 by the system of direct taxation, and £50 by the system of loans, the wish to preserve his fortune unimpaired would induce him to discharge it by increased labour and diminished expenditure, and in the first case he will try to save £1,000, in the second only £50. Want of mental perspective prevents men from seeing that a tax of one million a year is as burdensome as one of twenty millions at once, and, perhaps too, the idea that part of the burden in the former case may fall on posterity induces them to prefer the method of borrowing. The ablest defenders of the Funding System admit that in regard to National Wealth, the plan of raising supplies within the year is much to be preferred. It not only stimulates the nation's energies, but dissuades it from indulging and continuing in expensive contests without good cause.

1845—1850

Having established the immediate taxation system on this pinnacle of apparent superiority, McCulloch at once proceeds to throw stones at it. One objection is the loss to persons who can ill afford to part with their capital, and cannot easily recoup themselves by increased energy or diminished expenditure; such are landlords and manufacturers, for example. Of course these people may themselves borrow in order to pay their tax, and so reduce their contribution to, say, £50 per annum, instead of £1,000 down, but then the Government, if it had borrowed for them, could have obtained much better terms, especially when it borrowed for thousands of others at the same time; but the grand argument against it is the sudden and oppressive addition to the weight of taxation. There comes a point at which increased taxes mean not increased energy and economy, but a decline of both; a shock sufficient to cause such a decline should be avoided, but short of such a catastrophe, the conclusion is that the immediate taxation system is the best.

The alarm felt by Hume and Smith at the proportions of the National Debt, and their predictions of the mischief it would occasion, have, McCulloch considers, been falsified only by the rapid increase and perfection of new inventions which he would ascribe, to a great extent, to the stimulus occasioned by increased taxation.

The increase of the National Debt in England was due not so much to the unsettled state of the Government in England, which made borrowing the only way of raising money, but to the political ideas of the time. Bolingbroke, Swift, and other Whigs advocated it in order to secure the support of the monied interest, but, apart from this, the *res dura et regni novitas* made it the only possible way of raising money. The mistake made was in not abandoning or confining the practice in the time of George II., when the Government was comparatively secure.

The Debt and Funds of England. By P.O.Z. 1850.

Says of the Fundholders—"What security have these "people for their money? None! What security have "they for the payment of the interest of their money? "Political opinion, and the collection of Taxes!"

1857

A Select Collection of Scarce and Valuable Tracts and other Publications on the National Debt and the Sinking Fund.

150 Copies of this volume were printed for private distribution by Lord Overstone, and edited by J. R. McCulloch.   **1857.**

    I. An Essay on Public Credit.   1710.

    II. A Letter to a Friend, in which is shown the Inviolable Nature of Public Securities.   1717.

    III. An Essay on the Public Debts of this Kingdom.   1726.

    IV. A State of the National Debt, as it stood 24th December, 1716, &c., compared with the Debt at Michaelmas, 1725.   1727.

    V. A Defence of an Essay on the Public Debts of this Kingdom, &c., in answer to "A State," &c. (No. IV.)   1727.

    VI. Representation of the House of Commons to H. M. Geo. II., showing the State of the National Debts in 1716 and 1726.   1728.

    VII. Of Public Credit. By David Hume.   1752.

    VIII. An Account of the National Debt, from Blackstone's Commentaries. Book I. cap. 8.   1773.

    IX. An Appeal to the Public on the Subject of the National Debt. New Edition. By R. Price, D.D., F.R.S.   1774.

1857—1859

X. Extracts from the "Challenge;" or, Patriotism put to the Test in a letter to the Rev. Dr. Price.

By Jos. Wimpey.   1772.

XI. Note on the Sinking Fund established by Mr. Pitt in 1786. (See under date.)

XII. Considerations on the Annual Million Bill, and on the Real and Imaginary Properties of a Sinking Fund.   1787.

XIII. An Enquiry concerning the Rise, &c., of the National Debt of Great Britain and Ireland.

By R. Hamilton.   1818.

Another volume of the Overstone Collection of Tracts is referred to under "1857" in the B. of E. section. The contents of these two are dealt with, individually, under their respective dates. The rest of the set, although valuable and extremely interesting, bears on subjects beyond the scope of this bibliography.

The National Debt Financially Considered.

Edward Capps.   1859.

This essay won the £200 prize offered through the Society of Arts by Mr. H. Johnson. The first part of the work gives a brief historical sketch of the Debt and the Sinking Funds, &c.

The second section is devoted to the consideration of various schemes for reducing the Debt.

After commenting in a helpless sort of way on Terminable Annuities, he comes at length to a most extraordinary idea of his own, viz., to pay off the Debt by selling land lots in the Colonies. Whatever the Colonies may have thought about this notion thirty-eight years since, they would probably now differ from Mr. Capps, and might prefer to discharge their own debts, if they could, before performing the disinterested action he recommends.

1871—1889

NATIONAL DEBTS. By R. D. Baxter. 1871.

Gives much information in a condensed form. The annual charge per head of the Japanese for their Debt in 1870 was one halfpenny, and that of the British, fifteen shillings and ninepence, 378 times greater.

AN ACCOUNT OF THE OPERATIONS UNDER THE NATIONAL DEBT CONVERSION ACT, 1888, AND THE NATIONAL DEBT REDEMPTION ACT, 1889. By Edward Walter Hamilton. 1889.

A popular and attractive account of the greatest operation of the kind in history. Prefixed are letters from the author (now Sir E. W. Hamilton, and then and now Financial Secretary to the Treasury), to the Chancellor of the Exchequer, and the Chancellor's (Mr. Goschen's) reply. An extract from the latter will show the official and authoritative character of the book. "I am glad you have "written an account of the recent financial operations," writes Mr. Goschen, "for it will be interesting to have "the story told from beginning to end, and it could only "be so told by one who was behind the scenes all the time."

The Stocks which the Chancellor proposed to deal with were the Consolidated Three per Cent. Annuities, the Reduced Three per Cent. Annuities, and the New Three per Cent. Annuities. The two first could be redeemed on a year's notice; the last was redeemable at once, without notice. The aggregate amount of these three Stocks was about £558,000,000, but to this was added another £34,000,000, representing the Stock sunk in a Chancery Annuity. Mr. Hamilton shows that although these Stocks had stood well above par for a considerable time, their market price was, nevertheless, kept abnormally low by the fear of conversion or redemption. In the course of 10 years, he says, three Railway Debenture Stocks had risen about 24 per cent., Consols barely 6 per cent.; Metropolitan 3 per cent. Stock, irredeemable until 1941, was standing at $103\frac{1}{2}$, Consols averaged for the month of February, 1888, only 102. The prices of other Stocks are examined with a similar result. "It was therefore "evident," says Mr. Hamilton, "from the relatively large

1889

"rise in prices of other first-class securities, that the British Government was deriving no corresponding advantage from the vast increase of capital seeking investment. In short, British Credit was not being turned to the best account. 'The Champion Stock of the world,' as Mr. Goschen called Consols, "was being passed in the race, . . . and in view of all the circumstances, Her Majesty's Government were justified in making some proposals, which would not only lighten the burdens of the country, but would likewise, by terminating a period of suspense and delay, conduce to the interests of all who held or dealt in the Public Debt."

It was determined to offer holders of the 3 per cents. a New Stock, bearing interest at $2\frac{3}{4}$ per cent. until 1903, when it would automatically become a $2\frac{1}{2}$ per cent. Stock, and be guaranteed against redemption or further reduction until 1923. The success of the scheme was immediate. So rapidly did the conversion proceed that, within a fortnight of the passing of the Act, considerably over 400 millions Stock had been exchanged, and the resources of the Bank of England were taxed to the very utmost in dealing with the enormous mass of work, some particulars of which are given. About 550 millions were converted altogether.

Next year the balance of £12,000,000 left unconverted was dealt with. $18\frac{1}{2}$ millions were paid off in cash, $8\frac{1}{2}$ millions Redemption Money remaining unreceived on the 3rd of October, 1889, became New Consols through the Automatic operation of a provision in the Redemption Act, and the residue, belonging mainly to public departments, was partly exchanged for New Stock, and partly left in abeyance as a Book Debt.

THE FOUNDER, WILLIAM PATERSON.

WILLIAM PATERSON, the son of a small "Laird," was born in the parish of Tinwald, Dumfriesshire, in April, 1658. His biographer, Bannister, establishes this date by reference to his will, executed July, 1718, in which Paterson states himself to be sixty years and three months old. As is often the case with great men, he seems to have imbibed his religious principles from his mother, who appears also to have influenced his political views. It was the effect of this early maternal training which afterwards separated him from the Episcopalians and Jacobites, amongst whom a paternal relative, the last Archbishop of Glasgow, was an energetic leader.

He was also connected with Sir Hugh Paterson who, in 1715, was attainted of treason for his support of the Pretender.

About 1675 he came to England to avoid the persecutions then going on in the North against Presbyterians, and found shelter at Bristol with an aged female relative of his mother.

His hostess, on her decease, which occurred shortly after his arrival, left him a legacy, with which he seems to have started on his mercantile career.

Some writers have regarded him as a buccaneer, others as a missionary; but there seems, as yet, no good evidence to show he was either. There is little doubt that he was a merchant, as described by Anderson in his "History of Commerce." In 1681 he was admitted by "redemption" to the Merchant Taylors' Company, and was on the livery in 1689. This mode of becoming a freeman of the Company implies a mercantile standing.

About 1685 he visited Amsterdam, and haunted the various coffee-houses there, at that time much frequented by English Whigs. The city was then one of the largest centres of commerce, and the opportunity of meeting traders of all nations was, no doubt, eagerly embraced by Paterson, and had great influence in widening his views and freeing him from insular prejudices.

In 1686 he went to Prussia, and unsuccessfully endeavoured to obtain the assistance of the Elector of Brandenburgh for his Darien scheme.

Before 1687 he had connections with New England, as appears from one of his letters written from Darien in 1699, and published in Boston at the time. His first wife was the widow of a Presbyterian minister in that colony, whose name was Bridge. His second wife was Mrs. Hannah Kemp, another widow, whom a lampoon of the period describes as keeping a coffee-shop in Birchin Lane.

With the support of Sir John Trenchard he founded the Hampstead waterworks for the better supply of North London with pure water from reservoirs south of the Highgate and Hampstead hills. There exists abundant evidence to show that Paterson was by no means the unknown and vulgar adventurer he has been frequently represented to be; on the contrary, although his beginnings were small, by the time he was forty he seems to have had wealth, influence and culture, and, above all, a reputation for strict integrity. We now come to that period of his life in which he was engaged in the foundation of an institution whose stability has, during the two hundred years of its life, become proverbial. In 1691-2 he was a witness before a Committee of Parliament appointed to investigate measures to meet the urgent public needs. Bannister gives the following extract from the Journals, Vol. X., page 621, 18th January, 1692: "Mr. Foley reports "from the Committee appointed to receive proposals for raising "a sum of money towards carrying on the war against France, "on *a fund of perpetual interest*, that there were several "persons interested in the 'Bankers' Debts' ready to take for "their debts, and a new loan of an equal amount, a perpetual "yearly interest of six per cent. by Act of Parliament."

"When this Committee first met, a paper was brought "forward proposing that, on settling a yearly rent of £65,000, "one million should be advanced. Sixty thousand would be "for interest and £5,000 to Trustees for management, so "as the subscribers may be Trustees and *their Bills of* "*Property should be current*. In this case they offer to "advance £200,000 to *be ready as a Bank*, to exchange such "current bills as should be of right to be exchanged, the "better to give credit thereto and make the said bills the "better to circulate; so as they be allowed £5 per cent. for "the said £200,000 for the first year only.

"The Committee were of opinion not to receive any proposal
"which required making the bills of property current, so as to
"force them as payment on any without their consent.

"But they acquainted Mr. Paterson, who made this
"proposal, that they would receive any proposal to advance
"one million on a perpetual fund of interest, to be in the nature
"of a purchase, where they might assign their interest as they
"pleased to any one who consented thereto. Mr. Paterson
"said he believed the gentlemen would come up to that, and
"not insist on having the Bills made current. . . . . .

"He believed himself and some others might come up to
"advance £500,000. Various other proposals were made,
"but nothing was proposed to the Committee on which they
"could rely."

Although this brings us very near the Bank, it was not till three years afterwards that the seed bore fruit, and then chiefly through the instrumentality of Charles Montague, afterwards Earl of Halifax. Montague, who at the time was one of the Commissioners of the Treasury, took up Paterson's scheme as a means of strengthening the national finances, and carried it successfully through Parliament. He was rewarded for this service by the Chancellorship of the Exchequer. Montague also was brought into sympathy with Paterson, through their mutual opposition to the Land Bank and other inconvertible paper schemes which came from the Tory side.

In the "Wednesday's Club Papers," series 1717, *q.v.*, (page 63), Paterson, to a certain extent, has told the tale of the Bank himself:—

"I can but think, said Mr. Speed, how joyful men in
"those circumstances must have been at hearing of the
"proposition of the Bank.

"The proposition of the Bank, said Mr. May, was first
"made in the months of July and August, 1691, and was so
"far from being well received that nothing was permitted to
"be done in it for three years after, and then but lamely
"neither, and far from the extensive nature and other public
"advantages concerted in the proposition. What then did
"they say to it? said Mr. Speed. Some said it was a new
"thing and they did not understand it, said Mr. May, besides,
"they expected an immediate peace, and so there would be
"no occasion for it." After various comments, Mr. May said,

"At last (1694), with much ado, they ventured to try the
proposition of the Bank, although not so as to affect the
general credit for the better, so much as at first designed,
but only as a lame expedient for £1,200,000. . . . . .
Had it not been for the Queen, who insisted on the express
orders from the King, then in Flanders, the Commission
had not passed, consequently, notwithstanding all the former
pains and expense of private men about it, there had still
been no Bank.

"To the point in hand, said Mr. Jones, from the chair.
How did it go with the subscription to the Bank, and what
were the consequences? Notwithstanding the still continued
opposition, the subscription was completed in about ten days,
said Mr. May, and the whole money paid into the Exchequer
without deduction in so many weeks.

"After which the Bank not only relieved the managers
from their processions to the city to borrow money on the
best and nearest public securities at ten and twelve per cent.
per annum, but likewise gave life and currency, to double
or treble the amount of its capital, to other branches of the
then public credit, and so, under God, became the principal
means of the success of the campaign in the following year,
1695, particularly in reducing the important city and fortress
of Namur, the first material step to the peace concluded at
Ryswick two years after. The which peace, precarious as it
was, considering the then low and distracted circumstances
of the nation, could not, humanly speaking, have been even
so obtained without some such seasonable relief and support
as that of the Bank proved to be."

Though Paterson was the ruling spirit amongst the
founders, he only remained on the Board of Directors about
a year. The exact reason for his so soon quitting it has
not yet been found out. Sir W. Scott and Chambers both
seem to think that his colleagues, having gained his
experience, wanted his room. It seems impossible, in the
first place, that so reputable a body of men should have acted
meanly, or, again, could have been so short-sighted as to
throw over a man of his high standing and ripe experience.

It is noteworthy that in the "Wednesday's Club Papers"
Paterson says simply "he went away," assigning no reason.
The writer of this notice would suggest that chagrin or
disgust were most probably the reasons for his withdrawal.

That he felt deeply the absence of special recognition of his services in connection with the Bank is certain. On 4th April, 1709, he wrote from Westminster to Lord Treasurer Godolphin, enclosing a petition to Queen Anne, in which he sets forth, " That your petitioner first formed and proposed " the scheme for relieving the public credit by establishing " the B. of E., but that, notwithstanding the signal success of " that institution for the public service, and his unwearied " endeavours in promoting the same through all manner of " opposition, from 1691 to the full establishment thereof in " 1694, never had any recompense for his great pains and " expense therewith." By the death of his friend Michael Godfrey, the Deputy-Governor, he lost his principal supporter on the Board, and on a motion he wished to carry was outvoted by his co-directors. This occurrence, coupled with the neglect of his deserts, doubtless caused him no slight disappointment and mortification. He had probably too much self-respect to make a fuss, and the earliest convenient sale of his £2,000 Bank Stock (his qualification as Director) and his consequent retirement from the Board would most likely have been the natural course, under the circumstances, to a man of Paterson's temperament.

The rapidity with which he turned to the Darien scheme shows how he longed for fresh fields for his creative energy. It is a pity that he so soon left the B. of E., as in the re-coinage troubles that quickly came, his clear views and incisive mind would have been invaluable.

This is not the place to discuss the Darien scheme; it need only be said that evidence is available to show that it was well planned, and that Paterson, through his self-devotion, nearly lost his life. The reason of its terrible collapse was principally the scandalous way in which the Government withdrew their support and left the wretched colonists in the lurch in a thoroughly helpless state. Paterson's foresight is well shown in the following anecdote. Knowing the bad effects of alcohol in tropical climates, he prevailed on many of the Darien colonists to take a pledge to abstain, in consideration of being paid the value of the saving to the Company by their abstinence. Thus far Paterson's prevision. By the 15th Article of the Treaty of Union the principal sums (with £5 per cent. interest thereon) due to the proprietors of the African and Indian Company of Scotland, the workers of the Darien enterprise, took precedence of all other public debts of Scotland, and were payable by the Commissioners of the "Equivalent Fund." Years after the collapse one of the surviving colonists, who had taken the pledge, applied for the amount of arrears due to him on account of the non-consumption of his spirit rations while in Darien; although his nationality is not given, it is scarcely doubtful.

Paterson lost £10,000 in the Darien business. Oddly enough, however, it was chiefly through the affair that failed, and not through the great success, that he received his long deferred reward. On 18th March, 1707, the first United Parliament of England and Scotland resolved "that Paterson "ought to be paid all the sums owing to him by the African "and Indian Company." On 4th April, 1709, he still prays for speedy relief, and says "that, through continued troubles "and expensive proceedings, he was unable to subsist or "extricate himself from the debts and difficulties" he was in. In 1713 a strong Committee of the House of Commons awarded him £18,241 10s. 10¾d.; the Lords, however, threw out the Bill, and it was not till 1715 that the award was at last made.

In 1703 he endeavoured to form a public library of works on commerce, and offered his own collection of books on that subject to the nation. His offer and the catalogue of the library is in the Harleian Collection, British Museum, and is valuable to students of commercial bibliography of the 17th century. In his will, executed 1st July, 1718, he leaves to various relations £6,400, and £1,000 to Paul Daranda, of London, merchant, an old friend, whom he made his executor. He seems rather doubtful as to residuary estate, as he says: " I give the surplus of my estate, if after payment of my " debts any such shall be, to be divided among the said " legatees in proportion to every person's sum which is " bequeathed." Notwithstanding the money which we must suppose him to have possessed when the will was made, in December, 1718, we find him, only five months afterwards, writing a begging letter to Lord Stanhope referring to the " difficult juncture of his affairs," and craving assistance. The end of one of the busiest lives of the time was now near, and his death took place in January, 1719.

He seems to have left his house in Queen Square, Westminster, some time during the preceding year, and this fact, and the letter to Lord Stanhope, together with a reference to him in a contemporary journal as "a man famous for "his skill in calculation without having greatly enriched "himself," all tend to show that he was at any rate not overburdened with riches. Some day, perhaps, some piece of evidence may be unearthed to show how much of the award he really did receive. Judging by the will, he must have been paid a good part of it, and he seems to have enjoyed a fair measure of public esteem, and to have had a certain amount of influence with important personages up to the end of his career.

The subjoined list of works, known to be his, or with good reason attributed to him by Bannister, places him before us as a man of enormous industry and varied interests. His works are most clearly written, and the insight displayed in them exhibits him not only as a sort of "Zeitgeist" in himself, but as far ahead of his time. There are few men who deal with the deeper questions of sociology with such knowledge and freshness as to keep our attention rivetted to the page two centuries after the ink from their pen has ceased to flow; but Paterson is one of them.

Owing to his keen interest in all the advanced movements of his day, and his marked faculty for seeing beyond the mere phenomena right into the realities, a really exhaustive biography would be an important work, and would open up the rich historical soil of a period when the seeds of modern thought and life were developing with a growth whose vigour was only equalled by its rapidity.

A List of Paterson's Works.

- 1690. Portions of a Tract on the Government of the West Indies.
- 1691. Plan of the Hampstead Water Works Company.
- 1692. Evidence before the House of Commons on Public Loans.
- 1694. Two Tracts on the B. of E.
- 1695. The Scottish Act of Parliament on Darien.
- 1695. Letters on Darien.
- 1696. Tracts on Coin and the Stoppage of the B. of E.
- 1699. Report on the Disasters of Darien.
- 1700. Paper on the Revival of the Darien Colony.

List of Paterson's Works—*cont^d*.

- 1700. Tract on the Social Progress of Scotland, or his Proposals of a Council of Trade. (Attributed, by some, erroneously to John Law.)
- 1701. Tract on the National Debt.
- 1701. Tract on Auditing the Public Accounts.
- 1701. Memoir on Free Trade and on British Settlements in Central America.
- 1702. Paper on Taxation.
- 1706. Wednesday Club Dialogues on Legislative Unions of Great States.
- 1706. Letters on the Union.
- 1706. Paper on the Revenue of England and Scotland.
- 1709. Letters to Lord Treasurer Godolphin on Taxation.
- 1710. Paper on Toleration.
- 1716. Paper on Redeeming the National Debt.
- 1717. Wednesday Club Dialogues on the Results of the Union and on Redemption of National Debt.

THE FIRST GOVERNOR.

Sir John Houblon belonged to a Huguenot family; his father was a merchant, and an elder of the French Protestant Church in London. The son joined the father in his business, which was chiefly in the Spanish trade, and became what the world calls successful.

He was Sheriff and Alderman in 1689, and was knighted by William III. at the Lord Mayor's feast in that year, on 29th October, O. S. = 9th November, N. S. He was a Whig, and, with Sir John Fleet, in 1692, was put up by his party for the Mayoralty in opposition to two Tory Aldermen. Fleet, who was the senior, was selected. Houblon was chosen Lord Mayor on 28th September, 1695. The Grocers' Company payed the expenses of his "show."

He stood high at this time, as, in 1693, he had been made a Lord of the Admiralty, and held office till June, 1699; on 21st June, 1694, too, he had been an original subscriber for £10,000 Bank Stock, and had been made the first Governor of the Bank. Honours still fell thick upon him. In 1696 he became Master of the Grocers' Company; and it was by his influence, probably, that Grocers' Hall was selected as the Bank's premises, when they removed from Mercers' Hall, where one or two meetings had been held. In December, 1696, he delivered a statement of the Bank's affairs to the House of Commons. In 1703 the House of Lords placed him on the Commission of Accounts. His Spanish agent sent him early intelligence of the raising of the siege of Gibraltar by the French and Spaniards. The central front of the present building in Threadneedle Street was built in 1734, on the site of premises formerly in his occupation. He died in January, 1711, and was buried in S. Benet's, Paul's Wharf.

His brother, Sir JAMES HOUBLON, was also a member of the original Directorate. He was an Alderman, and represented the City in Parliament from 1698 to 1700, and died in the following year. The Houblon family were much connected with the B. of E. An Abraham Houblon was a Director in 1694, and a Sir Richard Houblon in 1713.

THE FIRST DEPUTY-GOVERNOR.

Michael Godfrey was the son of a merchant of London, and nephew of Sir Edmund Berry Godfrey, whose murder, laid at the door of the Papists by the notorious Titus Oates, caused a great sensation a few years before the Bank was founded. Michael and his brother Peter were both merchants, and, to their father's horror, of a rather speculative turn of mind.

Godfrey seems to have been an energetic and popular man of business, and was a staunch supporter of Paterson in his project of the new Bank, and became its first Deputy-Governor.

On 15th August, 1694, he was chosen one of a Committee, 15 in number, for the framing of by-laws for the B. of E. On 16th May, 1695, a General Court was held, at which Peter Godfrey, his brother, was also elected a Director. At this time it was proposed to establish a Branch B. of E. in Antwerp, to facilitate the payment of the troops in Flanders.

M. Godfrey, in conjunction with Sir James Houblon (the Governor's brother) and Sir William Scawen, who afterwards became Deputy-Governor, were deputed to proceed to the seat of war to make the necessary arrangements with the King, who was besieging Namur. They were honoured by an invitation to dinner in the King's tent.

On 17th July, 1695, Godfrey, who was standing close to the King, in the trenches, was killed by a ball from the town. His personal value to the Corporation was shown by a fall of £2 per cent. in the price of Bank Stock at the news of his death.

In 1695 he published "A Short Account of the B. of E." (*q. v.*), which has been frequently reprinted, and is so well and freshly written that it is still interesting reading.

His favourite adage was: "We cannot do good to "ourselves but by doing good to others." This indication of his character would lead us to conclude that he was not only a brilliant commercial genius, but also a good man. He stands high amongst Bank worthies. His brother Peter survived him about twenty years.

ABRAHAM NEWLAND.

Up to the end of this present century, Newland seems to be the only servant of the Bank whose name has been handed down to posterity in that capacity. Many of its employés have achieved distinction in Literature, and in the Arts and Sciences, but their names are known only as writers or painters, musicians or scientists. Newland's name passed into the colloquial English of the time, a Bank Note being known in, and long after, his day as an "Abraham Newland."

During the period of the restriction of cash payments at the end of the last and the beginning of this century, when a piece of gold coin was scarcely ever seen, Newland's signature on the Notes was always before the public eye, and he became, in his way, almost a national celebrity. After the return to cash payments and the withdrawal of the small Notes, an "Abraham Newland" became a rarity. A year or two ago a curiosity-dealer sold a genuine £1 Note to a friend of the compiler for ten shillings, and hoped he would not think it dear! Had he taken it to the Bank he would, of course, have been paid twenty shillings for it.

Newland was born 23rd April, 1730, in Castle Street, Southwark, his father being William Newland, a miller and baker, at Grove, Bucks.

He entered the Bank in 1748, and after a faithful service of thirty-four years, rose to the position of Chief Cashier in January, 1782. He seems to have been a man of cheerful disposition, not over fond of publicity, but doing his duty unobtrusively, and accumulating money whilst jogging along the even tenor of his way.

The exposure of the "Astlett" frauds in 1803, was, however, a severe blow to him. The criminal had unhappily been a protégé of Newland, and held a good position in the Bank's service, doubtless in no small measure owing to his old friend's recommendation. He showed his gratitude to the Bank and his benefactor by embezzling a large number of Exchequer Bills, and was in due course tried and convicted.

At the first half-yearly meeting of the Bank Stock proprietors after his conviction, the Governor stated that the total loss to the Bank would be about £320,000. "About "£78,000," he added, "have been employed in sources from "which the Directors think they shall be able to recover, and "they were determined to prosecute for that purpose; that the "loss amounted to nearly the entire dividends of the half year, "but the affairs of the Company were in so prosperous a "condition that they should be able to divide as usual."

This affair of Astlett seems to have affected the old man's health, which from this time gradually declined.

Owing to the quiet way in which Newland lived, it is difficult to get hold of any anecdotes illustrative of his character; the following one, however, is believed to be authentic.

Early one morning, as Newland, who lived in the Bank, was walking in the garden before breakfast, one of the porters came up in haste and told him that there was a poor man waiting who was in a great state of mind as to cashing a £10 Note. At so early an hour, the clerks not having yet arrived, and the offices not being opened, this was, of course, impossible. "Bring him to me," said Newland. He told the man that if he wanted the ten sovereigns he would have to wait for at least an hour, but, under the circumstances, he would help him and let him have £9 10s. for his Note. After some hesitation, and not without grumbling at the hardship, the man took the offer and went his way, whilst Abraham, with a self-satisfied chuckle, pocketed the Note bearing his superscription. On going into his office, his first act was to hold up the Note with an air of pride, saying, "See what the early bird has caught," and, addressing the man nearest to him, "Be so good as to cash this for me." One man after another backed out of the job and left Newland still holding his Note. "Hullo! what's the matter; why don't you do it?" Then the answer came, "Well, sir, there is no doubt of it, it's a forgery."

Until 22nd September, 1807, he had slept at the Bank for five-and-twenty years without being away for a single night. He then moved to 38, Highbury Place, under the care of his old friend Mrs. Cornthwaite, and remained with her there till his death.

When the end was evidently near, he received a present of a ham from an acquaintance to whose good offices he had before owed nothing. Abraham saw the real object of the gift, and at his next meeting with the donor, raised his finger with a significant gesture, and said, "It won't do, my dear sir, I tell you it won't do."

His Doctor, in one of his last visits, found the old fellow deeply absorbed in the newspaper, and gently expressed his surprise at finding Newland still interested in the affairs of this world. He replied with a smile, "I am only looking at the paper in order to tell what I am reading to the world I am going to." Shortly afterwards he died, very quietly, on the 21st November, 1807, and was buried in the churchyard of S. Saviour's, Southwark.

He is said to have suggested the following verse for his own epitaph:—

> "Beneath this stone old Abraham lies,
> Nobody laughs and nobody cries :
> Where he has gone, and how he fares,
> No one knows and nobody cares."

He left behind him a large sum of money, the largest, most probably, that any Bank Clerk has hitherto left, or is likely to leave, for the then constantly recurring issues of Government Stock gave many opportunities for "a little business," in those easy-going days. It seems to have been usual for the employés of the Bank both to receive a considerable share of the commission paid on the issue of a Loan, and to apply for, and be allotted, large sums of the new Stock, which they were, probably, always able to dispose of at a premium. The accompanying extract from a contemporary newspaper shows that he did not forget his old friends, either in the Bank or out of it.

"*The late Mr. Abraham Newland.*

"The Will of Mr. Newland has not yet been registered, " but we are enabled to state its principal contents.

"Mr. Newland died worth £200,000 in Stock, besides " £1,000 per annum arising from estates, and he disposed of it " in the following manner :

"To Mr. Henry Hase (now Chief Cashier), Mr. Rippon
"(Second Cashier), Mr. Attwood and Mr. Bross £500 each
"as executors. To Mrs. Cornthwaite, housekeeper to the
"deceased, the income from £60,000 Consols and his personal
"effects, a legacy of £5,000 in cash down, the house and
"furniture at Highbury, and his horses and carriage.

"To Mr. Hase, £250 per annum, arising from the Broad
"Street Annuity (money lent by Mr. Newland to the parish,
"and when the annuity shall cease the principal to be repaid),
"and £700 Consols; Mr. Rippon, 700 guineas; Mr. Bross,
"700 guineas; Mr. Attwood, £10,000. To each of the family
"of the Goldsmids, eight in number, £500 to purchase rings.
"To the gentlemen belonging to the Chief Cashier's Office,
"about twenty in number, from £30 to £100 each, with about
"two exceptions. To the Porters at the Bank and Lodge
"from £10 to £50 each, and to the domestics of the deceased's
"household the like sums. The residue of the property is
"left amongst the relatives of the deceased; among them is a
"Chelsea Pensioner, who during Newland's life received £50
"per annum, has been left £100 per annum; a farmer's
"servant at Hornsey, who had not partaken of the testator's
"bounty during his lifetime, has been left £300 per annum."

One feels curious to know what the offence of the excluded individuals in the Chief Cashier's office could have been. If the whispers of the day were true, Newland and the Goldsmids had many a time been serviceable to one another, and had not been totally uninterested in the operations of the "Bulls" and "Bears."

The above seems to be the testamentary disposition of a man who, at any rate, had endeavoured to remember his friends. On the whole, Abraham Newland seems to have been a careful, kindly, self-contained man.

The following stanzas, written about the year 1800, were sung at a dinner of the B. of E. Company of the Civil Service Rifle Volunteer Corps, in February, 1879;—this act of commemoration shows that the present generation have not forgotten

ABRAHAM NEWLAND.

O, there ne'er was a name so blazon'd by fame,
   Thro' the air, or thro' ocean, or thro' land,
As the one that is wrote upon every Bank Note,
   And you all must know Abraham Newland.
      O, good Abraham Newland!
      Note-able Abraham Newland!
I have heard people say: "Sham Abram you may,"
But you mustn't sham Abraham Newland.

If for fashion or arts you should seek foreign parts,
   Not a jot does it matter where you land;
Christian, Turk, Jew or Greek, the same language they speak,
   That 's the language of Abraham Newland.
      O, great Abraham Newland!
      Noted Abraham Newland!
Tho' with compliments cramm'd, you may die and be ——!
If you haven't an Abraham Newland!

All the world is inclined to think Justice is blind,—
   Lawyers know very well they can view land, —
But lord! what of that? She'll blink like a bat
   At the sight of an Abraham Newland.
      O, crisp Abraham Newland!
      Bank Note-ified Abraham Newland!
Tho' Dame Justice, 'tis known, can see thro' a millstone,
She can not see thro' Abraham Newland!

Then, those patriots who bawl for the good of us all—
   Worthy souls!—Here, like mushrooms, they strew land,
Tho' as loud as a drum, still as mice they become,
   If attacked by stout Abraham Newland.
      O, stout Abraham Newland!
      Note-orious Abraham Newland!
Not an argument's found in the world half so sound
As the logic of Abraham Newland!

In writing these Bibliographical Notes, reference has been made to Bannister's *Writings of Paterson*; *Pennant's London*; *Luttrell's Brief Relation*; *Dictionary of National Biography*; *Life of Abraham Newland*; and contemporary sources.

CHRONOLOGICAL SUMMARY OF EVENTS
From 1694.

1694. Charter issued 27th July, to continue to 1st August, 1705. B. of E. installed at Grocers' Hall.
1695. Michael Godfrey, first Deputy-Governor, died 17th July in the trenches at the siege of Namur. Bank of Scotland founded by J. Holland.
1696. Bank Notes at 20 per cent. discount. Suspension of payment owing to recoinage difficulty.
1697. Charter extended to August, 1710. Bank Stock, by law, made personal, not real, property, and profit thereon exempted from taxation. Exchequer Bills issued, said to have been invented by Montague, Earl of Halifax. (*see* 1796).
1698. Darien Expedition. New East India Company founded.
1699. Bank Stock, highest 119, September; lowest $101\frac{3}{4}$, January.
1700. Bank Stock, highest $148\frac{1}{4}$, March; lowest $124\frac{1}{2}$, December.
1701. Charles II. Debt to Goldsmiths first treated as National Debt.
1702. Amalgamation of New and Old East India Companies.
1703. Bank Stock, highest $138\frac{3}{4}$, September; lowest 129, January.
1704. £1 Notes issued by Bank of Scotland.
1705. Charitable Corporation Fund established; sort of Savings' Bank somewhat on the Scotch Cash Credit system. It only lasted about three years.
1706. B. of E. exempted from usury laws. Old Gloucester Bank opened by James Wood.
1707. Renewal of Charter to August, 1732.
1708. B. of E. Capital doubled. Act 6 Anne passed, prohibiting the Issue of Notes in Great Britain by any body of more than 6 persons, other than the B. of E.
1709. A call of 15 per cent. on Bank Stock in February.
1710. A call of 10 per cent. on Bank Stock in December. First Lottery subscription at B. of E.
1711. South Sea Company formed.
1712. Drummond's Bank established.
1713. Extension of Charter to 1742.
1714. Legal rate of Interest lowered to 5 per cent. from 6 per cent., at which latter rate it had been fixed in 1651.
1715. Subscriptions for Government Loan first received at B. of E. (1 George I., cap. 19). Act passed " For relieving " William Paterson out of the ' Equivalent Money' for " what is due to him."
1716. Walpole's Sinking Fund created. Interest on South Sea Co.'s Debt reduced to £5 per cent.

1717. Guineas made current at 21s., their specie value being only 20s. 8d.
1718.
1719. William Paterson died in January.
1720. South Sea Bubble commenced. Issue S. S. Stock at 2000 falling to 400 in September. Bank Stock 260. E. India Co. Stock 445.
1721. Unsuccessful attempt to start a National Bank in Ireland.
1722. First formation of Reserve Fund "The Rest." The practice in emergencies hitherto had been to make calls on the proprietors.
1723.
1724. Interest on Debt from Government to B. of E. reduced to £4 per cent.
1725.
1726. First £3 per cent. Loan raised.
1727. Royal Bank of Scotland founded by Proprietors of Equivalent Fund.
1728.
1729. Cash Credits instituted by Royal Bank of Scotland.
1730. Reduction of E. I. Co.'s Annuity and of Debt to South Sea Co.
1731. £3 per cent. Stock: highest 99, lowest 91.
1732. One p.m., Thursday, 3rd August, foundation stone of new building in Threadneedle Street laid by Sir Edward Bellamy, Governor. G. Sampson, Architect.
1733. Walpole's Excise Bill defeated.
1734. Thursday, 5th June. Business first transacted at Threadneedle Street. Act passed against Stockjobbing.
1735. Fuller, Banbury & Co. commenced business.
1736. Bank of Copenhagen established.
1737. £3 per cent. Stocks at 107. Unsuccessful attempt to reduce Interest on all Redeemable Stocks to £3 per cent.
1738. 14th December, B. of E. first issued Post Bills payable 7 days after sight, to give chance of stoppage of payment in case of Mails being stolen by highwaymen or others.
1739. £3 per cent. Stock: highest $106\frac{1}{4}$, lowest $96\frac{1}{2}$.
1740. } In England, at this time, Cheques seem to have been scarcely used at all. In the Acts giving Charters to various Banks
1741. } mention is made only of Notes.
1742. Charter renewed to August, 1764.
1743. Meyer Rothschild born.
1744. Alexander's Bank at Ipswich founded. Pitt takes Office.
1745. Run on the B. of E. caused by rebellion in the North. B. of E. Notes paid in silver (sixpences, &c.) 1140 Merchants signed declaration that they would accept B. of E. Notes in payment.
1746. Call of 10 per cent. on Bank Stock. British Linen Co. founded.
1747. £3 per cent. Stock: highest 86, lowest 81.

1748.	£3 per cent. Stock: lowest 76, highest 91.
1749.	Conversion £54,000,000. Pelham, Chancellor of Exchequer. £4 per cents. reduced to £3 : 10s. per cents.
1750.	£4 per cent. Debt from Government to B. of E. reduced to £3 : 10s. per cent. Cocks Biddulphs', Glyns', and Becketts' (of Leeds) Banks established about this date.
1751.	£3 per cent. Stock: highest 103, lowest 97.
1752.	Formation of £3 per cent. Consols and £3 per cent. Reduced Stocks. Act 25 Geo. II. cap. 27.
1753.	£3 per cent. Stock: highest 106¼, lowest 103⅛.
1754.	„ „ „ 104¾, „ 101½.
1755.	First Act for making Canals in England passed.
1756.	Commencement of Seven Years' War. Reduced £3 per cent. Stock: First dividend paid 5th January.
1757.	£3 : 10s. per cent. become £3 per cent., in accordance with the terms of Pelham's Conversion; also £3½ per cent. Debt from Government to B. of E. reduced to £3 per cent.
1758.	Legally settled that those who had given value for B. of E. Notes stolen from Mails were entitled to payment from B. of E. First forgery of £20 Note (smallest amount then in circulation) by R. W. Vaughan, linen draper of Stafford. Hanged.
1759.	First Issue of £15 and £10 Notes and Post Bills by B. of E.
1760.	£3 per cent. Stock: highest 85, lowest 75½.
1761.	The "Long Annuities" created.
1762.	Brindley completed Canal from Worsley to Manchester.
1763.	Panic in Hamburg and Amsterdam extending to London. B. of E. made advances amounting to £1,000,000. Dundee Banking Co. started.
1764.	Renewal of Charter till August, 1786.
1765.	£3 per cent. Stock: highest 92⅔, lowest 85.
1766.	Perth Banking Co. and Prescott's established.
1767.	£3 per cent. Stock: highest 92½, lowest 87¼.
1768.	„ „ „ 94¾, „ 87½.
1769.	Inventions of Watts' Steam Engine and Arkwright's Spinning Jenny made known.
1770.	Eastern Wing added to B. of E.
1771.	£3 per cent. Stock: highest 89, lowest 78¼.
1772.	Black Monday, 8th June, panic. Heale & Co., of Threadneedle Street, Bankers, failed. Robarts & Co. opened.
1773.	In the books of Messrs. Martin an entry appears "Quarterly "charge for use of Clearing Room, 19s. 6d."
1774.	Western Wing added to B. of E.
1775.	Institution of London Clearing House. Bankers prohibited from issuing Notes of less amount than 20s. 15 Geo. III. cap. 51.
1776.	Bankers prohibited from issuing Notes of less amount than £5.

1777. £3 per cent. Stock : highest $82\frac{1}{8}$, lowest $75\frac{7}{8}$.

1778. £3 per cent. Stock : highest $75\frac{3}{4}$, lowest $60\frac{3}{4}$.

1779. About this date the modern Cheque came into general use.

1780. "Gordon" Riots. Repulse of attack on the B. of E., since when the building has been protected at night by military guard.

1781. Charter extended to August, 1812. Church of S. Christopher-le-Stocks taken down. Legally decided that the B. of E. is not liable to pay forged Notes.

1782. Commercial Crisis commenced, and culminated in the Spring
1783. of this latter year. Bank of Ireland opened 25th June at S. Mary's Abbey, Dublin. The last nominee of the Tontine of 1692 died, aged 100.

1784. Navy £5 per cent. created.

1785. £3 per cent. Stock : highest $73\frac{1}{4}$, lowest $55\frac{1}{8}$.

1786. Pitt's Sinking Fund established, and Commissioners for the Reduction of the National Debt appointed. Rate of payment to B. of E. for Management of the Funded Debt fixed at £450 per million ; prior to this the rate had been £562 : 10*s*.

1787. Consolidated Fund formed by combining the Aggregate, General, and South Sea Funds. 27 Geo. III., cap. 13.

1788. Sir John Soane appointed Architect to B. of E.

1789. £3 per cent. Stock, highest $81\frac{1}{4}$; lowest $71\frac{1}{2}$.

1790. Issue of Tontine Loan of 1789 ; last survivor died 31st October, 1887.

1791. A new and distinct Sinking Fund established of One per cent. upon the Debt created in respect of future Loans. Allowance to B. of E. for management, arranged in 1786, sanctioned by Parliament.

1792. Run on the B. of E. latter end of this year and beginning of next (*see* 1797).

1793. £3 per cent. Stock : highest 81, lowest $70\frac{1}{2}$.

1794. First Issue of £5 Notes.

1795. Rotunda built by Soane.

1796. Exchequer Bills (*see* 1697) first circulated by B. of E.

1797. 26th February (Sunday). Order in Council for Restriction of Cash Payments, and, on 10th March, Notes of £1 and £2 were issued. In March, Spanish Dollars were put into circulation, a small head of Geo. III. being stamped on the Spanish King's neck. Bank Restriction Act passed 3rd May. Mutiny at the Nore. The following comparison shows the state of the Market.—

	Before the fall in 1792.		*April*, 1797,—
£3 per cent. Consols	$97\frac{1}{8}$	...	$47\frac{3}{4}$
£4 per cents. .	. $105\frac{5}{8}$	...	$60\frac{5}{8}$
£5 ,,	. 120	...	$72\frac{3}{4}$
Bank Stock	. 219		$121\frac{3}{4}$

1798. Land Tax made redeemable in £3 per cent. Stock. Bank Volunteer Corps formed.
1799. First English Savings Bank. "Benevolent Institution," started at Wendover by Rev. J. Smith.
1800. Renewal of Charter to August, 1833. Bank Notes at par. Gold at 77s. 10½d. per oz.
1801. Bank Notes at 8 per cent. Discount. Gold at 85s. per oz. Foundation Stone of present Stock Exchange laid in Capel Court, 18th May.
1802. Consolidation of Sinking Funds. Addington, Chancellor of the Exchequer.
1803. Astlett Frauds (see A. Newland). Bank of France instituted by laws not approved till 1808.
1804. Five Shilling Dollars issued by B. of E.
1805. Gold £4 per oz. Silver 5s. 5d.
1806. Directors' fees doubled.
1807. Abraham Newland retired from the Chief Cashiership of the B. of E. in September and died 21st November. Lord Henry Petty's Plan of Finance.
1808. Notes of Country Bankers taxed. Payment to B. of E. for management of Funded Debt reduced to £340 per million to £600,000,000, and to £300 per million beyond. Purchase of Life Annuities in connection with Government Stock established by Spencer Perceval.
1809. B. of E. adopted Bramah's Machine for numbering Notes.
1810. Bullion Committee. Gold £4 : 10s. per oz. Bank Notes at discount of 13 per cent. (or a £1 Note = 17s. 4d. only). Separate premises taken for Clearing House.
1811. Act passed making it a misdemeanour to take a B. of E. Note for less than its value. 9th July, B. of E. issues Silver Tokens for 3s. and 1s. 6d.
1812. Gold £4 : 18s. per oz. (Note = 15s. 11d.) Average price of Wheat in England and Wales, 155s. per quarter (some Dantzic Wheat fetched 180s.) £3 per cent. Stock : 55¼ to 63.
1813. Gold £5 : 10s. per oz. (Note = 14s. 2d.) Issue of £5 per cent. Exchequer Debentures. Sinking Fund modified by Vansittart, Chancellor of Exchequer.
1814. Gold £5 : 4s. per oz. (Note = 15s. or 25 per cent. Discount) July. Wheat 68s. Bank and other Volunteers disbanded.
1815. April, Gold £5 : 7s. per oz. June 9th, £5 : 5s. per oz. June 18th. Waterloo. June 20th, £5 per oz. July 7th, £4 : 14s., and October 13th, £4 : 3s. per oz.
1816. Consolidation of English and Irish Exchequers. Act (56 Geo. III. cap. 60) passed to transfer Unclaimed Stock to National Debt Commissioners.
1817. Loan of £3,000,000 by Bank to Government. Gold £3 : 18s. 6d. per oz. Temporary partial resumption of Cash payments. B. of E. prosecuted in this year 142 persons in connection with forgeries.

1818. Transfers of Stock first authorised from England to Ireland. B. of E. gave up the practice of detaining forged Notes, simply returning them to the holders stamped with the word "Forged." Conversion of £27,000,000. Vansittart, Chancellor of Exchequer. Holders of £100 £3 per cent. Stock offered £88 in £3 : 10s. per cent. Stock, and on payment of £11 in money, to a further sum of £12 in the new Stock. £3 per cent. Stock : highest 82. lowest 73.

1819. Act passed for gradual resumption of Cash payments ("Peel's "Currency Bill").

1820. 352 Convictions in respect to forged B. of E. Notes and Post Bills ; 77 Capital convictions. and 275 for having forged Notes in possession.

1821. 1st May, complete resumption of Cash payments. Gold 77s. 10½d. per oz. £3 per cent. Stock : highest 78¾, lowest 68¾.

1822. Conversion of £152,000,000 Navy £5 per cents. to £4 per cents. Vansittart, Chancellor of Exchequer. £3 per cent. Stock : highest 83, lowest 75½. Many B. of E. clerks pensioned on account of the suppression of £1 and £2 Notes.

1823. Transfers of Stock from Ireland to England first authorised. Last Lottery drawn. B. of E. purchases "Dead Weight "Annuity" running for 45 years.

1824. Conversion of £76,000,000 £4 per cent. to £3 : 10s. per cent. F. J. Robinson, Chancellor of the Exchequer. Trial of Fauntleroy, the forger ; hanged 30th November ; altogether, the replacing Stock, legal expenses &c., cost B. of E. £360,000.

1825. £5 per cent. Loyalty Loan of 1797 converted to £3 per cent. Consols (£133 : 6s. 8d. Consols for each £100 Stock), or paid off at par. December, panic, run on B. of E. A box of £1 Notes accidentally found, and issued with the gold, had great effect in restoring confidence. Altogether, 70 Banks stopped payment.

1826. Up to this time, £10 was the amount of the lowest cheque permitted to be drawn ; now, £5 was allowed. Branches of B. of E. first established. Manchester, Swansea and Gloucester Branches opened. Statute enacted making the institution of Joint Stock Banks legal outside the 65 miles limit. Assimilation of English and Irish Currencies.

1827. B. of E. opens Branches at Birmingham, Liverpool, Bristol, Leeds and Exeter.

1828. Sinking Fund limited to a quarter of the actual surplus of revenue. Newcastle Branch B. of E. opened.

1829. "Old Sinking Fund" established. Goulburn, Chancellor of Exchequer. Annuities for Terms of Years, so called, created. Hull and Norwich Branch Bs. of E. opened. Thomas Maynard last person executed for forgery at the Old Bailey.

1830. Conversion £153,000,000 New £4 per cents., optional at par, to £3 : 10s. per cents., or at 70 to £5 per cent. Only half-a-million was converted on the latter terms. £3 per cent. Stock : highest 91¼, lowest 77½.

1831. Reform Riots. £3 per cent. Stock: highest 84¾, lowest 74¾.
1832. Committee of Secrecy on B. of E. Management of Tontine and Life Annuities transferred from B. of E. to National Debt Commissioners.
1833. Renewal of B. of E. Charter, in which was inserted Declaratory clause permitting Joint Stock Banks in London.
1834. Public Moneys paid direct into B. of E. instead of into Exchequer. Branch Bs. of E. opened at Plymouth and Portsmouth, and that at Exeter closed in May. London and Westminster Bank started. One-fourth part of Debt due from Government to Bank paid off.
1835. £20,000,000 raised for compensation to Slave-owners, partly in £3 per cent. Stock, with long annuity, and partly in £3 : 10s. per cent. Stock.
1836. London Joint Stock Bank founded.
1837. Forgery reduced from a capital to a transportable offence.
1838. Stockbrokers expelled from Rotunda, which has since been used by the B. of E. itself.
1839. Commercial Crisis. Foundation of the Union and of the London and County Banks.
1840. Committee appointed on Banks of Issue.
1841. Removal of Clearing House to present premises in Post Office Court.
1842. Reimposition of Income and Property Tax.
1843. In May, B. of E., at request of Stock Exchange Committee, notified that no transfer would be allowed after 1 p.m., and that the future days for public transfer would be Tuesday, Wednesday, Thursday and Friday.
1844. Bank Charter Act passed, separating Banking from Issue Department, and enacting that the privileges of the Bank were to continue till twelve months' notice, to be given after 1st August, 1855, and repayment of debt due from public. Conversion of £248,000,000 £3 : 10s. per cent. into £3 : 5s. per cent. for 10 years (1854), and then to £3 per cent. only. £3 per cent. Stock: highest 101¼, lowest 96¼. Leicester Branch B. of E. opened.
1845. Railway Mania. Act 8 & 9 Vict. cap. 62 passed to pay Dividends Unclaimed for 10 years, and upwards, to the Commissioners for the Reduction of the National Debt.
1846. Repeal of the Corn Laws.
1847. Commercial Crisis. 25th October, the Government suspend the Bank Charter Act of 1844. £3 per cent. Stock: highest 94, lowest 78¾.
1848. £2,000,000 raised in £3 per cent. Stock at £114 : 8s. 5d. per cent.
1849. Gloucester Branch B. of E. closed 28th February.
1850. Institution of Clerks' Library in the B. of E., and of the Clerks' Fidelity Guarantee Fund.
1851. £3 per cent. Stock: highest 99, lowest 95½.

1852. £3 per cent. Stock: highest 102, lowest 95¾. Norwich Branch B. of E. closed 31st May.
1853. Attempted Conversion of £3 per cents.: highest 101. Exchequer Bonds and New £2 : 10s. and £3 : 10s. created.
1854. Joint Stock Banks admitted to Clearing House. Usury Laws abolished.
1855. New form of Bank Note adopted. Failure of Strahan, Paul & Co.
1856. Western Branch B. of E. opened 1st October.
1857. Panic. Act of 1844 suspended 12th November.
1858. Committee on Bank Charter Act.
1859. Swansea Branch B. of E. closed in February. Commercial crisis in April.
1860. Long Annuities expired. Payment to B. of E. for Management of Funded Debt reduced to £300 per annum per million up to £600,000,000, then £150 per million.
1861. Post Office Savings Banks opened. Act passed (24 Vict. cap. 3) making Charter determinable on twelve months' notice, and repayment of debt due from public.
1862. Theft of Bank Note Paper from the makers' mills. Many forged Notes soon about. Forgers tried and convicted in January, 1863.
1863. Red Sea Annuity created.
1864. B. of E. joined Clearing House in April.
1865. £3 per cent. Stock: highest 91¼, lowest 87.
1866. Panic, 10th May, failure of Overend, Gurney & Co. B. of E. rate of discount £10 per cent. £3 per cent. Stock: highest 90¼, lowest 85⅜. 11th May, Government suspended Bank Act of 1844. Bank Volunteer Corps enrolled as "K" Company of C.S.V.R. Corps.
1867. Terminable Annuities created. Allowance to B. of E. for Management of Unfunded Debt fixed at £100 per million.
1868. Dead Weight Annuity expired 31st March.
1869. National Purchase of Telegraphs.
1870. National Debt Act passed (33 & 34 Vict. cap. 71); this consolidates and amends the Acts of 1816 and 1845, the first enacting the payment of Stocks and Dividends thereon, and the second of Unclaimed Dividends only, to the National Debt Commissioners.
1871. 25th May, Sir John Lubbock's Bank Holiday Act passed.
1872. Leicester Branch B. of E. closed in February. Clearing Houses opened at Manchester and Newcastle.
1873. Cheque Bank started.
1874. £3 per cent. Stock: highest 93½, lowest 91½.
1875. Financial crisis. A. Collie & Co., Sanderson & Co., and J. C. im Thurm & Co., Bill Brokers, failed. New Sinking Fund Act. Purchase of Suez Canal Shares. Formation of 50th (afterwards 25th) Middlesex V. R. Corps (Bank Porters and Mechanics) attached to C. S. V. R.

1876. Foundation of Imperial Bank of Germany (formerly of Prussia).
1877. Treasury Bills created.
1878. Financial pressure. City of Glasgow Bank failed.
1879. Institute of Bankers founded. London and Westminster Bank made "Limited."
1880. Great Depression in Trade.
1881. Trustee Savings Banks Deficiency Annuity created.
1882. Entrance to B. of E. in Princes Street opened.
1883. Creation of Chancery and "Rolling Annuities" in place of £70,000,000 Stock cancelled.
1884. Attempted Conversion of £3 per cent. £19,000,000 to £2 : 10s. per cent., and £4,000,000 to £2 : 15s. per cent., 1905. Childers, Chancellor of Exchequer. £3 per cent. Stock: highest 102¾, lowest 99$\frac{5}{16}$.
1885. New Sinking Fund and portion of Terminable Annuities representing Capital suspended for the year.
1886. Royal Commission on Currency.
1887. Conversion of India £4 per cent. to £3 : 10s. per cent. Local Loans Stock created.
1888. National Debt Conversion. Goschen, Chancellor of Exchequer. £3 per cent. Stock: highest 103¾. New Law Courts Branch B. of E. premises opened in Fleet Street.
1889. Redemption of £3 per cent. Stocks. The total amount of £3 per cent. converted to £2 : 15s. per cent. Stock, under the Conversion Act of 1888 and the Redemption Act of 1889, was £565,000,000. Dividends payable quarterly.
1890. November Commercial crisis (Baring & Co.) Panic averted by prompt action of B. of E. taking the leading part, in conjunction with other Banks, in the formation of a Guarantee Fund. "Accumulative Dividends" introduced.
1891. Amalgamation of Prescott's and Dimsdale's Banks. Vagliano case decided by the House of Lords in favour of the Bank, and decisions of Judge and of the Court of Appeal overruled.
1892. Bank Act passed (55 & 56 Vict. cap. 48). Allowance to Bank for management of National Debt adjusted to meet quarterly payment of dividends. Interest on Permanent Debt reduced from £3 per cent. to £2 : 15s. per cent. Amalgamation of Parr's and Alliance Banks.
1893. Banking Crisis in Australia.
1894. Finance Act passed altering Death Duties. Bank Rate of Discount £2 per cent. from February (till September, 1896).
1895. The Baring Liquidation completed in January. Great speculation in South African enterprises.
1896. Supplemental Charter as to internal affairs of B. of E. under Bank Act of 1892. £2 : 15s. per cent. Consols: highest 113¾. Barclay & Co. Limited, formed by amalgamation of Barclay, Ransom & Co., with Goslings, and thirteen country Banks.

INDEX OF NAMES.

Addington, Lord, 80, 82
Allardyce, A., 27
Althorp, Lord, 71
Arbuthnot, G., 87
Arnott, Charles, 51
Ashman, Thomas, 135
Atkinson, J., 32, 44, 66
Attwood, T., 56

Baker, Henry, 98
Balbernie, A., 39
Banfill, S., 44
Bannister, Saxe, 92
Baring, Sir F., 26, 30
Baring, Bros., 113
Baring, Thomas, 84
Barnard, Sir John, 129
Bath, Pulteney, Earl of, 126
Baxter, R. D., 155
Bennison, W., 75
Birch, J. W., 35
Bird, Robert, 136
Blackstone, 133
Blake, William, 37
Boase, Henry, 34, 40
Bollmann, E., 56
Bosanquet, Charles, 38, 43
Bosanquet, J. W., 79
Boyd, W., 30, 149
Box, George, 136
Bradbury, Henry, 85
Brand, Thomas, 56
Brickwood, John, Junior, 147
Brookes, Henry, 93

Campbell, D. F., 84
Capps, Edward, 154

Castlereagh, Lord, 41
Cazenove, John, 71
Chalmers, George, 45
Chamberlen, Dr., 4
Chambers, A. H., 55
Chesterfield, Lord, 131
Chevalier, M., 84, 92
Clare, George, 116
Clay, Sir William, 80
Cleeve, Bourchier, 131
Cobbett, William, 50
Cobden, Richard, 92
Cochut, P. A., 85
Cohen, B., 118
Collins, C. M., 100
Comber, W. T., 49
Congreve, Sir W., 58
Cooke, E., 53, 56
Corbaux, F., 118
Courtenay, T. P., 149
Cradocke, F., 2
Crauford, Lieut.-General, 49
Crawford, R. W., 97
Crump, A., 95
Currie, Captain J. P., 117
Curtis, Alderman, 141

Defoe, Daniel, 123
Doubleday, Thomas, 82
Drummond, H., 58, 78
Dunbar, C. F., 116

Egan, Pierce, 62
Elibank, Lord, 23, 131
Eliot, F. P., 40
Exeter, J., 63

Fairman, W., 148. 149
Fauntleroy, 62
Forbes, Sir William, 92
Fortune, T., 32
Francis, John, 83
Fry, Thomas, 141
Fullarton, John, 81

Galton, S. T., 47
George II., 128
Gerbier, Sir B., 1
Giddy, D., 44
Gilbart, J. W., 79. 83. 104
Gilbert, D., 53
Godfrey, M., 5. 166
Goldsmid, J. L., 61
Gompertz, E. 59
Gordon, R., 73
Goschen, Rt. Hon. G. J., 118. 155
Gould, Sir N., 125. 127
Grant, J. P., 46
Grellier, J. J., 142
Grenfell, H. R., 35. 108
Grenfell, John, 47. 147
Grenfell, Pascoe, 48
Grenville, Lord, 67. 149

Hales, C., 28. 29
Hall, W., 56
Hamilton, Sir E. W., 155
Hamilton, Robert, 143
Hankey, Thomson, 108
Hardcastle, D., Junior, 80
Hawes, B., 80
Heathfield, R., 147
Hoare, Sir R., 21
Hooke, Andrew, 129
Horner, F. 40
Horsley Palmer, J., *see* Palmer
Horton, S. Dana, 100
Houblon, Sir John, 165
Houghton, J., 14
Howarth, W., 105
Hubbard, J. G., *see* Lord Addington
Hume, D., 22. 131
Huskisson, W., 44. 46. 52. 60. 61
Hutcheson, A., 125

Jevons, W. S., 98. 107
Johnson, Andrew, 84
Johnstone, Mr., 45
Joplin, T., 60. 61. 63. 76

King, Lord, 33. 34
Klaproth, J. 61

Lambe, S., 1
Langton, W., 98
Lansdown, Lord, 142
Lasalle, J. II., 33
Lauderdale, Lord, 57. 58
Law, John, 85
Lawson, W. J., 84
Leighton, J., 85
Lidderdale, Rt. Hon. W., 114. 115
Liverpool, Lord, 35. 49. 53. 56. 57. 59
Loyd, S. Jones, *see* Overstone
Luttrell, N., 86
Lyne, C., 57

McCulloch, J. R., 69. 81. 88. 90. 150
Macleod, H. Dunning, 94. 99. 113
Malagrowther, Malachi, 64
Marnière, J. H., 31
Martin, F., 94
Melbourne, Lord, 76
Merrick, L. V. E., 116
Michie, A. S., 104
Moore, R., 67. 73
Moray, R., 2
Morgan, William, 138. 141
Morrison, W. H., 76
Mundell, A., 68. 70
Mushet, R., 63

Newhaven, Lord, 137
Newland, A., 37. 167
Norman, G. Warde, 77

Overstone, Lord, 74. 75. 79. 81. 87. 93. 153
Oxford, Harley, Earl of, 124

Pagan, W., 94
Page, R., 80
Paget, Thomas, 60
Palmer, J. Horsley, 71. 74. 75
Parnell, Sir Henry, 36. 66. 70
Paterson, John, 94
Paterson, W. 3. 5. 16. 92. 94. 157
Patterson, R. H., 96
Payne, D. B., 48

Peel, Sir Robert, 55. 57. 60. 80. 81
Perkins & Fairman, 58
Petty, Lord Henry, 142
Phillipps, Sir John, 129
Phillips, Maberly, 118
Pitt, W., 28. 31. 44. 132. 138. 110
Playford, W. M., 105
Pope, Simeon, 141
Postlethwayt, J., 24
Postlethwayt, M., 24
Poulett Scrope, G., 67
Preston, T., 101
Price, Bonamy, 98
Price, Charles (Swindler), 33
Price, Sir Charles, 44
Price, F. G. Hilton, 98
Price, Dr. R., 132. 134. 136. 138
Prinsep, C. R., 49
Pulteney, Sir W., 26, 136
Pusey, P., 149

Quin, M. J., 72

Rae, George, 107
Raikes, R. M., 71
Rawdon, Lord, 25
Ricardo, D., 42. 43. 47. 59. 60. 62. 81
Rogers, J. Thorold, 111
Rogers, S., 61
Rooke, John, 149
Rose, George, 42
Rosse, Lord, 39. 43
Rutherford, A. W., 54

Scheer, F., 84
Scott, Sir Walter, 64
Scrope, G. P., 67
Senior, N. W., 68

Seyd, E., 96. 97
Sinclair, Sir J., 27. 38. 44. 67
Siordet, J. M., 44
Slater, Robert, 93
Smart, B., 52
Smith, T., 55
Stair, Lord, 136
Stanhope, Lord, 45

Tate, W., 79
Tatham, E., 28. 48. 138
Taylor, James, 66. 68
Taylor, John, 73
Thornton H., 32, 41
Tooke, T., 61. 67
Torrens, R., 76. 81
Turner, S., 57

Vansittart, N., 40. 59, 140

Wallace, Dr. R., 23
Ward, J., 82
Ward, William, 78
Webster, R., 97
Wellington, Duke of, 68
Wells, S., 71. 73
Western, C. C., 60. 61
Weston, A., 50
Wheatley, John, 36
Wigram, Clifford, 108
Wilson, A. J., 99
Wimpey, Joseph, 132
Winter, J. P., 70
Wolowski, L., 94. 95. 96
Wood, Charles, 81. 82
Wray, John, 54

Young, Arthur, 46

INDEX OF SUBJECTS.

	PAGE
Agriculture. (*Ricardo*)	59
American Monetary Conference	99
Annual Million Bill	137
Analysis of the Money Situation	39
Assurance Company. London	143
———— Royal Exchange	143
Bane and Antidote. (*S. Rogers*)	61
Bank Annuities, Analysis of. (*Ishman*)	135
BANK OF ENGLAND :	
Act of 1844. (*Brookes*)	93
———— (Petition against)	82
Apparent Dangers of	15
Arguments against prolonging	15
Bank at Paris equal to. (*Marnières*)	31
Barometer for 1855	85
Chancellor of Exchequer. (*Lord Althorp*)	71
Chart. (*Baker*)	98
Charter of. (1694)	25
— ———— (1742)	29
(1823)	61
(*Fullarton*, 1844)	81
(*Hawes*, 1844)	80
(*Joplin*, 1822)	60
(*Quin*, 1833)	72
— (*Torrens*, 1844)	81

BANK OF ENGLAND—*continued*.   PAGE

    Committees on. (1819) .   54
    ——————— (*Bullion*, 1810)   38
    ——————— (*Cazenove*, 1832)   71
    ——————— (*Cooke*, 1819)   56
    ——————— (*Evidence*, 1832) .   72
    ——————— (*Hales*, 1797) .   28
    ——————— (*Lord Liverpool*, 1819)   53
    ——————— (*Mundell*, 1832)   70
    ——————— (*Turner*, 1819)   57
  Conduct of   25
  Constitution of   4
  Contract of   19. 20

  Dangers and Mischiefs of   15
  Defended   12. 65
  Detention of Post Bill at. (*Smart*)   52
  Directors of   140

  Early Days of .   7. 11
  Engrafting Tallies   13
  Establishment of. (*Baring*) .   26
  Exchequer Bills   15

  Facts relative to   61
  First Nine Years of. (*Rogers*)   111
  Fund for Clerks' Widows .   36

  Government and   51
  ——————— (*Gompertz*) .   59
  ——————— (*Wells*) .   71
  Governors of. (*Sinclair*)   27

  Historical Sketch of. (*McCulloch*)   69
  ——————— Reply to. (*Parnell*)   70
  History of. (1797) .   27
  ——————— (*Fortune*)   32
  ——————— (*Francis*)   83
  ——————— (*Lawson*)   84

BANK OF ENGLAND—*continued*.   PAGE

    Interest Tables . . . 5
    Issues of. (*Gilbart*) 83
    ———— (*Mushet*) 63
    ———— (*Seyd*) 97

    Justified in their present course. (*Ward*.) 82

    Letters on . . 73
    Luttrell on 86

    Management of. (*Hankey*) 108
    Mystery of. (*Cobbett*) . 50

    Notes, an Injury 30
    ———— (*Galton*) . . . 47
    ———— Depreciation of. (*Ricardo*) . . 42
    ———— One Pound 68
    ———— Security and Manufacture of. (*Bradbury*) 85
    ———— Superfluous Issue of. (*Rosse*) . . 39
    ———— Vindicated. (*Arbuthnot*) . 87

    Organization of Credit and 95

    Paper System and 76
    Printed at . 97
    Profits of . . . 18
    ———— (*Ricardo*) 47
    ———— (*Arnott*) 51
    Proprietors. ———— ——— 46
    ———— ———— . 140
    ———— ———— . 66
    ———— (*Allardyce*) 27
    ———— (*Arnott*) 51
    ———— (*Payne*) 48
    ———— (*Ricardo*) . 47
    ———— (*Ward*) . 78
    ———— (*Winter*) . 70

    Reasons against continuance of 13
    Reasons for encouraging . 11

BANK OF ENGLAND—continued.   PAGE

 Remarks on 11. 14
 Reply to defence of 12
 Representation by Directors. (1819) 54
 Restriction Act 50
 ———— ———— (*Goldsmid*) . . 64
 ———— ———— (*Lasalle*) . . 33
 ———— ———— (*Wray*) 54

 Separation of Departments. (*Jones Loyd*) 81
 Short Account of. (*Godfrey*) . 5
 Solicitors. (*Smart*) . 52
 Solidity of 65
 Some Observations on. (1695) 7
 South Sea Co. . 17
 ———— ———— . 18
 Stock. (*Rogers*) 112
 Stock Exchange . 59
 Subscription for 16
 Suspension of Cash Payments. (*McCulloch*) . 90

 Table. (1844-1857) . 98
 Tallies 13
 Tokens . 47

 Vade Mecum . . . 24
 Volunteer Corps. (*Preston*) 101
 ———— ———— (*Merrick*) 116

 Wolowski on . 95
 Women of England . 149
 Working of. (*Hankey*) 108

Bank of Ireland. (*Collins*) . 100
———— ———— (*King*) 33
Bank Post Bill. (*Smart*) . . 52
Bank Stock. (*See* Bank of England)
Bank Stock Proprietors. (*See* Bank of England)
Banker, Country. (*Rae*) 107

	PAGE
Bankers, London. (*Price*)	95
Banking and Currency. (*Crump*)	95
Banking, Debate on. (*Wood*)	81
——— in England and Scotland. (*Joplin*)	63
——— in Ireland. (*Gordon*)	73
——— in Northumberland. (*Phillips*)	118
——— History of. (*Dunbar*)	116
——— (*Gilbart*)	104
——— (*Lawson*)	84
——— (*Macleod*)	113
——— in North of England. (*Phillips*)	118
Houses, Memoirs of. (*Forbes*)	92
——— Principles of	76
——— (*Hankey*)	108
Provincial	49
Reform. (*Wilson*)	99
Banque d'Angleterre. (*Wolowski*)	95
Banques, La Question des. (*Wolowski*)	94
Banks and Bankers. (*Martin*)	94
(*Page*)	80
Banks, Country. (*Mushet*)	63
———	65
Joint Stock. (*Gordon*)	73
and Paper Credit. (*Wallace*)	23
and Paper Money. (*Elibank*)	23
——— (*Hume*)	22
Bimetallism. (*Grenfell*)	108
(*Morrison*)	76
Bibliography of	99
Brief Relation. (*Luttrell*)	86
British Plantations, Currencies of	19
"British Press"	51
Bullion Question. (*Giddy*)	44
——— (*Gilbert*)	53
——— (*Ricardo*)	59
——— (*Thornton*)	41
Bullion Report. ———	46
——— (of 1810)	38
——— (*Horner*)	40
——— (*Ricardo*)	43

	PAGE
Challenge. (*Wimpey*)	132
Chancellor of Exchequer, Letter to. (*Hubbard*)	82
Circulating Medium	50
——————— (*Crauford*)	49
——————— (*Scrope*)	67
Circulation, State of. ———	65
——— Paper. (*Baring*)	26
——— Bullion and. (*Chalmers*)	45
——— Chart of. (*Galton*)	47
——— Management of. (*Jones Loyd*)	79
——— Improved. (*Sinclair*)	67
City, The	84
Civil Service Rifle Volunteer Corps. (*Merrick*)	116
Civis	45
Clearing House. (*Howarth*)	105
——————— (*Tate*)	79
Coins of the Realm. (*Liverpool*)	35
Collection for Improvement of Husbandry, &c. (*Houghton*)	14
Commerce, as it was, &c.	41
Common Sense on Bullion Question	46
Conference, International Money. (*Horton*)	99
Consolidated Fund. (*Morgan*)	138
Copper Coinage. (*Grenfell*)	47
Corn, Low Price of. (*Ricardo*)	47
Country Banker. (*Rae*)	107
Country Banks. (*Mushet*)	63
———————	65
———————	68
Course of Exchange. (*Blake*)	37
——————— (*Lauderdale*)	57
Courier, Letters to	62
"Craftsman"	19
Credit, Commercial. (*Marnière*)	31
——— Currency. (*Scrope*)	67
——— Individual	46
——— Public. (*Oxford*)	124
——— Theory of. (*Macleod*)	113
Crisis. (1836)	76
——— Baring. (*Macleod*)	113
Crown Bank	11

CURRENCY

	PAGE
Act of 1844. (*Torrens*)	81
Banking and. (*Gilbart*)	79
— — (*Joplin*)	76
(*Price*)	98
Bank. (*Comber*)	49
Case of. (*Moore*)	67
Change of. (*Scott*) .	64
Circulating Medium and	49
Country and. (*Hubbard*)	80
Depreciation of	39
—— .	41
— — —— (*Eliot*) .	40
— (*Huskisson*)	52
- (*Rutherford*)	54
(*Paget*)	60
Economical and Secure. (*Ricardo*)	47
Exchange and. (*Blake*)	37
Fallacies. (*Taylor*) .	73
Increase of .	65
Investigations in. (*Jevons*)	107
Joplin on	62
Late and Future. (*Hall*)	56
Management of .	63
Metallic. (*Bosanquet*)	79
———— (*Morrison*)	76
Overstone Tracts on	87
Paper	19
——	39
—	46
— (*Elibank*)	23
(*Hume*)	22
(*Klaproth*)	61

CURRENCY—continued. PAGE
    Paper. (*Parnell*) 66
    ——— (*Senior*) 68
    ——— (*Taylor*) 73
    ——— (*Wallace*) . 23
    Present State of 46
    Principles of. (*Drummond*) . 58
    Reflections on . 79
    Reform in. (*Slater*) . 93
    Remarks on Reports of Committees . 54. 55

    Scotch. (*Scott*) 64
    Silver. (*Prinsep*) . 49
    ——— (*Rutherford*) 54
    State of. (*Jones Loyd*) 75
    ——— (*Rosse*) . 43
    ——— (*Tooke*) 64

    Thoughts on . 79
Currencies, Regulation of. (*Fullarton*) 81

Darien 161
DEBT :
    Account of. (*Blackstone*) . 133
    Appeal on Subject of. Remarks on . 132
    ——————— ——— (*Price*) 134

    Blackstone on 133

    Comparison. (1716-1725.) (*Pulteney*) . 126
    ——————————— (*Commons' Journal*) 128
    Conversion and Redemption. (*Hamilton*) . 155

    Enquiry in answer to "Facts," &c. (*Vansittart*) . 110
    Evils of . 150
    Extinction of . 150

    Facts respecting. (*Morgan*) . 140
    Financially considered. (*Capps*) 154
    Funds. . 152
    ——— (*Hutcheson*) 125

DEBT *continued*.	PAGE
General View, &c.	132
Government Debt	22
Hamilton, Sir E. W., on	155
Hamilton, Robert, on	143
History of	130
— (*Grellier*)	112
Interest on. (*Barnard*)	129
Liquidating. (*Heathfield*)	117
Nation, of the	136
National Capital and. (*Hooke*)	129
National Prosperity	137
Overstone Tracts on	153
Paying off. (*Bird*)	136
(*Box*)	136
Public	18, 22
— (*Elibank*)	131
(*Gould*)	125, 127
Redeeming the. (*Morgan*)	138
Redemption of. (*Corbaux*)	148
————— (*Hamilton*)	155
Reducing Interest on. (*Barnard*)	129
Reducing	18
———— (*Brickwood*)	147
———— (*Cheere*)	131
(*Newhaven*)	137
Remarks on Appeal, &c.	132
Sinking Fund	137
———— (*Boyd*)	149
———— (*Commons' Journal*)	128
———— (*Courtenay*)	119
———— (*Goldsmid*)	64
———— (*Gould*)	125
(*Grenfell*)	147

		PAGE
DEBT—*continued*.		
Sinking Fund. (*Grenville*)		119
————— (*Hamilton*)		111
————— (*McCulloch*)		132
————— (*Phillipps*)		129
State of the. (*Hamilton*)		143
————— (*Price*)		136
————— (*Pulteney*)		126
Tatham on		138
Taxes and .		130
Dictionary of Political Economy. (*Macleod*.)		91
Discount. Rate of . . .		60
Domestic Affairs in 1721		128
Dublin. Exchange between London and. (*McCulloch*)		91
East India Stock. (*Defoe*)		123
" Economist." Joplin in .		76
————— on Francis . . .		83
England, Financial History. (*Doubleday*)		82
————— Monetary History . . .		93
————— Pecuniary Credit of. (*Moore*)		73
————— Staple Commodities of. (*Gerbier*)		1
Equitable Adjustment. (*Huskisson*)		60
Exchange. Foreign. (*Goschen*) . . .		118
Exchange. 1797-1804. State of. (*McCulloch*)		91
Exchequer Bills		15
Finance. New System. (*Fry*)		141
Finance. Science of. (*Patterson*) . . .		96
First Nine Years of Bank of England (*Rogers*) .		111
Foreign Exchanges. (*Goschen*) . .		118
Forgery of Fauntleroy, Trial for. (*Egan*)		62
Freshfields. (*Smart*) .		52
Funded Property, Value of .		142
Funding System. (*McCulloch*)		150
Funds, Debt and .		152
——— Price of		50
——— Public .		128

	PAGE
"Globe" . . .	51
Gold Coinage Controversy. (*Crawford*)	97
— Depreciation of. (*Chevalier*)	84
Discoveries. (*Scheer*) .	84
— Fall in Value of. (*Cobden*)	92
Lack of . . .	46
Recent Supplies of. (*Johnson*)	84
Government and the Bank . .	51
— — — (*Gompertz*)	59
— — — — — (*Wells*)	71
Grocers Hall. (*Luttrell*)	86
Guineas an encumbrance	31
High Price of Bullion.	45
— — . — . .	47
— — (*Cooke*)	53
(*Ricardo*)	12
Real Cause of	57
Hints for Investors. (*Playford*) .	105
Husbandry and Trade. (*Houghton*)	14
Interest, Rate of. (*Rose*)	42
Interest Tables .	5
International Monetary Conference	99
Intrinsic Self-Gauging Coin. (*Congreve*)	58
Ireland, Banking in. (*Collins*) .	109
—— Bank of. (*Lawson*) .	84
Joint Stock Banks. . .	73
— — — (*Quin*) .	72
— — — ("*Times*")	91
Lack of Gold	46
Land Bank . . .	11
Loans, Terms of. (*Grellier*) . . .	142
London Bankers, Handbook of. (*Price*)	98
Lord Protector, Observations to. (*Lambe*)	1
Lotteries .	29
Mercers' Chapel, New Bank at. (*Luttrell*)	86
Mississippi Scheme. (*Cochut*)	85

	PAGE
Monetary Conference. (*Horton*)	99
——— Legislation. (*Webster*)	97
——— System, Prevalent Errors. (*Norman*)	77
Money Crisis. (*Bennison*)	75
——— Derangements. (*Ward*)	78
——— Market. (*Exeter*)	63
——— ——— (*Jones Loyd*)	75
——— ——— (*Palmer*)	74
——— ——— (*Torrens*)	76
——— ——— Primer. (*Clare*)	116
——— and the Mechanism of Exchange. (*Jevons*)	98
——— Mystery of	93
——— Scarcity of. (*Tatham*)	18
——— System of England. (*Taylor*)	66
——— Theoretic Discourse on. (*Gompertz*)	59
——— Theory of. (*Wheatley*)	36
——— ———	44
"Morning Post"	39
National Bank, Establishment of a. (*Ricardo*)	62
National Debt. (*See* Debt)	
——— Debts. (*Baxter*)	155
Northumberland, &c., Banking in. (*Phillips*)	118
Note on Currency. (*McCulloch*)	90
——— London and Dublin Course of Exchange. (*McCulloch*)	91
Old Lady of Threadneedle Street	70
"Old Patch"	33
Origin of Paper Money. (*Klaproth*)	61
Orphans' Fund	5
Overstone Tracts on Currency	87
——— ——— National Debt	153
Paper against Gold. (*Cobbett*)	50
——— Credit. (*See* Currency.)	
——— Currency.	"
——— Money	"
Paterson, Works of	163
Patriots in Arms. (*Preston*)	101
Patriotism put to the Test. (*Wimpey*)	132

	PAGE
Pitt's Sinking Fund. (*McCulloch*)	132
Political Economy, Dictionary of. (*Macleod*)	94
Political Economy, Literature of. (*McCulloch*)	81
Poor, Number of	40
Preface Examined	39
Preliminary Tracts .	1. 2. 3
Privy Council Order	28
Progressive Value of Money. (*Young*) .	46
Promissory Notes. (*Clay*)	80
Protection to Agriculture. (*Ricardo*)	59
Provincial Banking	49
Public Affairs. (*Pulteney*)	136
———— Credit .	124
———— (*Hume*)	131
———— - Creditors	129
———— Debt. (*See* Debt)	
———— Finances. (*Morgan*)	141
———— Funds. (*Pope*)	111
———— Revenue. (*Postlethwayt*)	24
———— Securities	124
Question Monétaire. (*Wolowski*)	96
Question re-stated (1812)	46
Report of Committee on High Price Bullion. (*See* Bullion)	
Restriction of Cash Payments	33. 34. 64. 78
Resumption of Cash Payments	32. 55. 56. 57. 58. 67
Revenue, &c. of United Kingdom. (*Wills*)	73
Scotland, Bank of. (*Lawson*)	84
Scotland, Banking in. (*Joplin*)	60. 63
———— (*Parnell*)	66
Securities, Public .	124
Seigniorage. (*Seyd*)	96
Siderographic Plan. (*Perkins and Fairman*)	58
Silver Currency. (*Mundell*)	68
———— (*Prinsep*)	49
———— (*Rutherford*)	54
Silver, Price of	16
Sinking Fund .	64

	PAGE
South Sea Stock. . .	17, 18
——— ——— (*Hutcheson*)	125
State of Exchange between Dublin and London. (*McCulloch*)	91
Stockjobbers, Villainy of. (*Defoe*)	123
Suspension of Cash Payments. (*See* Bank of England)	
Sword Blade Co.	13
Taxation and Funding System. (*McCulloch*)	150
Theory of Credit. (*Macleod*)	113
Threadneedle Street, Old Lady of . .	70
"Times" Letters to	39, 45, 72, 91
Union of Great Britain. (*Paterson*)	16
Volunteers Corps, Bank. (*Merrick*)	116
——————————— (*Preston*) .	101
Villainy of Stockjobbers detected. (*Defoe*)	123
Wealth and Currency. (*Grant*)	46
Wednesdays' Club. (*Paterson*)	16

Printed at the Bank of England, by Walter J. Coe.

www.ingramcontent.com/pod-product-compliance
Lightning Source LLC
Chambersburg PA
CBHW020822230426
43666CB00007B/1061